Elijah
A MAN OF LIKE NATURE

by Theodore H. Epp

Founder

Back to the Bible

Grace Gospel Press
Duluth, Minnesota

Elijah: A Man of Like Nature
by Theodore H. Epp

Originally published in 1965 by The Good News
Broadcasting Association, Inc.

Front cover image courtesy of FreeBibleimages.org

ISBN: 978-1-939110-04-6

GGP
Grace Gospel Press
201 W. St. Andrews St.
Duluth, MN 55803
U.S.A.
www.gracegospelpress.com

Printed in the United States of America

Contents

Chapter 1

The Man Elijah

He was a remarkable man, so remarkable in fact that many Christians are inclined to look upon him as a kind of superhuman being. He lived a busy and useful life, and after his ministry was ended, God took him to heaven without his dying. Nearly a thousand years later, this man came back to earth and visited the Lord Jesus Christ on a mountain. According to some interpretations of prophecy, this same man will come back and minister on earth for a short time just prior to the Second Coming of Christ. His name is Elijah, a man whom we are inclined to set apart from ordinary servants of the Lord.

Such an estimate, however, is wrong. In the Book of James, we read: "Elias was a man subject to like passions as we are" (5:17). He was, after all, a human being like the rest of us. He had emotions and problems; he experienced the same ups and downs in his life that all of us face. *The Amplified Bible* says, "Elijah was a human being with a nature such as we have."

When we compare Elijah's life with David's, we find that David had many faults; yet he was called a man after God's own heart. Elijah, on the other hand, had very few weaknesses or sins recorded against him, but we are told that he was a man of "like nature" (RSV).

To harmonize such evaluations one must know and understand God's viewpoint. He knows our frailties and inabilities. We are only weak human flesh, something we must recognize if we want to keep a proper perspective on life. We must realize that in ourselves we are nothing and that any success we have in our spiritual life and ministry is due to God. Left to themselves, David or Elijah would have been complete failures, just as we would be. Both men became great because they trusted God. They committed themselves totally to do His will.

David, of course, knew how to deal with his faults in the light of God's truth and how to trust God for great things. We're told very little about Elijah's personal life, but a close study reveals that he was a human being like the rest of us. He was a man of like passions, or nature. The word "passion" in this context does not mean he had evil habits in the sense of gross sins, but he had feelings that we would expect in a human being. He was like us because he was afraid at times, and because of his fear he fled. Once he was discouraged almost to the point of death. He had the same needs and appetites the rest of us have, and he needed the support that only God can give. He was capable of suffering the same things we suffer, for he was only a man.

He was subject to the same frailties we are. He had the same nature, the same general kind of disposition all of us are heir to. But because he was taken from this world without dying, some of us hesitate to look at him as a pattern for our own spiritual lives.

From both David and Elijah we must learn to look not at the merits and abilities of a man but at the grace of God. In studying the lives of these great men, we are not unduly exalting them, rather we are exalting the greatness of God.

God has His own standard of greatness, and both David and Elijah measured up to that standard. Elijah was a righteous man. He was a man who prayed, a man who believed and a man who received answers from God. He received some outstanding answers to prayer, for he dared to believe what God told him.

His prayers of faith were outstanding; yet they do not illustrate the power of the prophet but the power of God in the heart of a man who was humble enough to believe Him.

Elijah's Name

Elijah's name means "Jehovah is my God." I believe this indicates that God was Elijah's strength and power. There is a vast difference between the two ideas that the Lord strengthens me and that the Lord is my strength. Paul emphasized this latter fact in Ephesians 6:10: "Finally, my brethren, be strong in the Lord, and in the power of his might." The apostle did not say that we should ask God for power to overcome this or to give strength for that, but we are to simply trust God to be the strength and power needed.

The Apostle Paul was perhaps the greatest exponent of this truth. Christ is made unto us whatever our need is. If we need strength, He is our strength. If we lack holiness, He is made unto us holiness. If we need righteousness, He is our righteousness. If we want life, He is our life. He is what we need.

Think of it this way. There is a difference between God's holding a shield before me and the fact that God is my shield. If God holds a shield before me, it will provide good protection, but if I realize that He Himself is my shield, I not only have protection, but also I will be more than a conqueror, for He is the divine victor.

One day I was reading Ephesians 1:13,14 where it says we are sealed with the Holy Spirit. I read it: "Ye were sealed *by* that holy Spirit of promise." A dear man of God corrected me by saying, "Brother, it does not say 'by'; it says 'with.' "This makes all the difference in the world. To be sealed by the Holy Spirit simply means that the Holy Spirit is the One who seals us. But if we speak of being sealed with the Holy Spirit, then He is both the instrument and the seal.

So seeing God as our strength and power is more than God's giving us peace; He is our peace. It is not only that God gives us strength to do something; but when we realize that God is our strength, then our resources are as limitless as God Himself.

Moses first surrendered himself to God at the age of 40 years. He was willing to become God's man to free the nation of Israel and take the Israelites out of the land of Egypt. He believed God and trusted Him for strength. Then he went out in the strength he trusted God for, but he accomplished very little. He killed an Egyptian and had to flee for his life. At the age of 80, after he had learned to know God in a much more personal way, he returned to Egypt. He did not ask God for strength; instead he returned in the strength of God. He let God undertake for him and recognized that he was merely an instrument in God's hand. The result was that the Israelites were emancipated and the Egyptian army destroyed. It is not a matter of great faith but of faith in a great God.

Elijah's Background

Elijah is first introduced to us as the Tishbite in I Kings 17. We are simply told that he was an inhabitant of Gilead. He came from the mountains of Gilead on the other side of the Jordan, possibly from a group that was something of an outcast group. He might have been from the tribe of Manasseh, for that area had been given over to Manasseh's descendants. They were a hill people, strong and rugged, dwelling in rude villages and hardened by life in the open air. The record indicates that Elijah was a powerful man physically, a person strong of mind and earnest in spirit.

His birthplace was the little town of Tishbeh, a small, obscure village in the mountains. His formal education was apparently not extensive, and of his early religious training we know next to nothing. He and his fellow Israelites were surrounded by enemies who were idol worshipers, but of Elijah we read: "I have been very jealous for the Lord God of hosts" (19:10). We gather from this that he was separated to God and desired to see God exalted. He must have had a thorough knowledge of the then existing Scriptures — the five books of Moses, Joshua and the psalms of David.

In his youth he must have pondered at length over the blight of sin that had degraded his people. Then, in his mature manhood, he saw how Jezebel, an ungodly woman from heathen Zidon, brought Baal worship into Israel. This was one of the darkest hours of Israel's history. Jezebel killed all the prophets of God she could put her hands on (18:4-13). Others had to flee for their lives. At one time Elijah thought he was the only prophet left until God told him that there were 7000 others who had not bowed their knees to Baal (19:18). They, however, were in hiding; they were not out working in the open for the Lord. Leading in idol worship were some 850 priests of Baal and of the goddess Asherah (18:19). This was the condition in Israel when Elijah's ministry began.

Elijah's Prayers

Elijah, as we have said, knew the Word of God, and he began to pray in the light of God's promises. He knew for example what Moses had stated in Deuteronomy 11:13-17: "And it shall come to pass, if ye shall hearken diligently unto my commandments which I command you this day, to love the Lord your God, and to serve him with all your heart and with all your soul, that I will give you the rain of your land in his due season, the first rain and the latter rain, that thou mayest gather in thy corn, and thy wine, and thine oil. And I will send grass in thy fields for thy cattle, that thou mayest eat and be full. Take heed to yourselves, that your heart be not deceived, and ye turn aside, and serve other gods, and worship them; and then the Lord's wrath be kindled against you, and he shut up the heaven, that there be no rain, and that the land yield not her fruit; and lest ye perish quickly from off the good land which the Lord giveth you."

Knowing the conditions God said would prevail if the Israelites practiced obedience and knowing what He had promised as judgment if they were disobedient, Elijah prayed that it would not rain. And it did not rain for a period of three and a half years. He prayed again that it would rain, and it did. These are good examples of the prayer of faith, for true prayer is claiming what God has said in His Word and asking Him to do as He has promised.

This is not the only time in the Bible where we find men of God going to the Word to find what God has said and then praying that God's Word will be fully carried out. True praying is simply taking God at His Word. This was how Daniel prayed: "In the first year of Darius the son of Ahasuerus, of the seed of the Medes, which was made king over the realm of the Chaldeans; in the first year of his reign I Daniel understood by books the number of the years, whereof the word of the Lord came to Jeremiah the prophet, that he would accomplish seventy years in the desolations of Jerusalem" (Dan. 9:1,2).

Daniel read in Jeremiah 25:11,12 that after 70 years of captivity, God would forgive His people and bring them back into their land. On finding this, Daniel prayed and fasted in sackcloth and ashes and confessed the sins of his people. Daniel expected God to act on the basis of His promise, and God did.

According to Daniel 10:2, the prophet was "mourning three full weeks." And then he stated, "I ate no pleasant bread, neither came flesh nor wine in my mouth, neither did I anoint myself at all, till three whole weeks were fulfilled" (v. 3). All this time he was praying. He was claiming the wonderful promise of God and waiting for assurance from God that the promise would be fulfilled.

This was how Elijah prayed also. We are told, "He prayed earnestly" (James 5:17). This literally means he prayed in prayer, or we might say, "He really prayed." His prayers were for the ears of God and not for the ears of people. Sometimes people remark, "So and so prays beautifully." Such prayers do not necessarily mean a thing to God. God hears prayer directed to Him and not to people.

Elijah did not know that there were still 7000 of God's servants remaining in Israel, possibly many of them hiding in the mountains. It was then that Elijah prayed that rain would cease to fall, which, of course, meant that drought would come. Some might think this was cruel. It would cause much suffering; even Elijah himself would be affected by it. This made no difference in his thinking, for he based his prayer on God's Word. Since God said this was good for His people if they left Him, then it would be good and not wrong to pray for such chastisement to fall on them. Its purpose was to bring God's people back to Him.

People need to know that God is the living God. In Elijah's day idols were worshiped, but they were dead objects. Someone needed to demonstrate that God was alive and powerful on behalf of His people. The Israelites needed to know that God's words were not empty utterances and that God would enforce His judgments. Up to that moment God had withheld judgment, but the time was ripe for God to show His hand (see Ps. 50:21,22).

Elijah prayed that God might be proven to be God before the eyes of His people. Would any of us dare to pray for judgment on the nations in light of the great sins and rebellion against God that we see everywhere? Elijah's prayer had quite an affect on him as well as others, but his praying was in the will of God and not on the basis of any personal grudge against others.

Have we prayed that the Lord would send an awakening at any cost? Perhaps we have asked God to send an awakening, but have we asked Him to do it at any cost?

I found myself praying that very way. Realizing something of the conditions of the day, I asked the Lord for an awakening at any cost. But I had to stop and think and consider. Could I honestly say, "At any cost"? We can at least tell the Lord that we are willing to be made willing to include the phrase "at any cost" in our prayers.

A spiritual awakening usually costs. Generally speaking, we are too selfish and unconcerned to pray for what will benefit us if it will cost suffering or trial, even if the goal will be pleasing to God. So many of us want to live unhindered so that we can go on accumulating money, filling up our bank accounts regardless of what happens to the lost. Perhaps we have not admitted this to ourselves, but that is the way we are by nature. We need to become concerned about what the Lord wants to accomplish in people's lives. What are national or personal reverses compared to God's glory and receiving His favor?

We in North America enjoy great prosperity today and are proud of it. But what if we were to face terrible economic reverses? A far greater loss than that, however, would be the loss of God's favor. Much more would be at stake than the loss of material things.

11

Chapter 2

Elijah, God's Prophet

Elijah had a true sense of values. As a prophet of God he knew what God desired, and he knew that what God desired was best for Israel.

We may think that we could never pray as Elijah did. Remember, God tells us he was a man of "like nature" (James 5:17, RSV). He was a human being like the rest of us, and he faced discouragement and dismay. The big difference between Elijah and most of us is that he boldly spoke out for God most of the time. A prophet had to walk alone, for few persons wanted to walk with him.

We read in II Timothy 3:5 of those who have a form of godliness but who deny its power. From such people we are to turn away. A true prophet of God will do that. By a prophet, we do not mean just one who foretells but one who tells out God's message. The prophets were not accredited by the religious systems of their day; they did not belong to those systems and did not seem to care that they were not endorsed by them. Very often the prophets were despised, persecuted and hated by religious leaders. The prophets had a special message and a mission to perform in arousing the slumbering conscience of God's people. They were also sent to comfort the people of God, but only a remnant believed them.

Even though Elijah came from an obscure background, he was called of God to stand before a king. "And Elijah the Tishbite, who was of the inhabitants of Gilead, said unto Ahab, As

12

the Lord God of Israel liveth, before whom I stand, there shall not be dew nor rain these years, but according to my word" (I Kings 17:1). Elijah could stand before Ahab because he first stood before God. To stand before God we must be cleansed by Christ's blood, reconciled to God through the sacrifice of Jesus Christ. We must constantly wait on God, being committed to Him, always ready to obey His slightest command. We must be at God's disposal to do little things or big things, whatever He calls us to do.

Our concern must be for the Lord and not for ourselves. This was Elijah's attitude, for he was jealous for the Lord God of hosts. Psalm 37:4 says, "Delight thyself also in the Lord; and he shall give thee the desires of thine heart." The word "delight" simply means to honor God, to find out what His pleasure is, to do His will and to speak the words that He has given. When we delight in Him, we have the right desires and are in a position where God can answer our prayers. God has promised that if we commit our way to Him and trust in Him, He will fulfill our desires.

Many people today talk about working for God. But our working for God is not most important. We must cooperate with God so He can work through us. This involves submission to His will. What I want means nothing; what He wants is everything. Samuel cried, "Speak; for thy servant heareth" (I Sam. 3:10).

There are times when I have found it necessary to refuse speaking engagements for the simple reason that they will rob me of time with the Lord. A few years ago I was invited by a friend to be with him during New Year's services. Before I was through, I had spoken seven times. I told my friend that I could never do it again, for it gave me no time for the Lord. We have time for only a 15-minute message on our radio broadcasts, but if it is to be of any value, we must prepare by being alone with God for two or three hours at the very least. Remember, the Lord Jesus Himself set the very best example of getting alone with God before ministering to people.

The Boldness of Elijah

Elijah was a man with a nature like ours. He had a remarkable ministry, but he was still human. He had special gifts from God and was set apart to perform a special ministry. The difference between him and us is due to the special work God had for him and the fact that he was fully submitted to God. When he relied on his own resources, he became as weak as a child. At one period in his life he was discouraged almost to the point of death. Renewed by God, he was as bold as a lion.

He dared to stand before King Ahab and pronounce the judgment of God on him and his kingdom. The prophet showed no hesitancy and expected God to do what He said He would. The basic principle behind this is given in the New Testament. In Mark 11:22,23 the Lord Jesus told us to "have faith in God." He continued, "For verily I say unto you, That whosoever shall say unto this mountain, Be thou removed, and be thou cast into the sea; and shall not doubt in his heart, but shall believe that those things which he saith will come to pass; he shall have whatsoever he saith." Jesus said this, and we are to believe it.

The first thing that Elijah did when he stood before Ahab was to remind the king that the God of Israel is a living God. Jezebel had brought Baal worship into Israel and had 850 priests leading in the worship of idols. So the first thing Elijah said was "As the Lord God of Israel liveth" (I Kings 17:1). As Job before him had said, "I know that my redeemer liveth" (Job 19:25). This was in direct contrast to the dead idol of Baal. It was also stated in preparation for what Elijah would prove at a later time on Mount Carmel. That event was still three years in the future, but it was the Living God who acted and demonstrated His power.

How great is our God? It is not so much a question of how great our faith is but rather how great our God is. That is the important thing. Elijah called on God to carry out His own pronouncements. God had stated that if the Israelites worshiped other gods, He would withhold rain from them. Elijah dared to believe God and pronounced judgment on

14

the basis of God's Word. He did not just pray, but he said, "As the Lord God of Israel liveth, before whom I stand, there shall not be dew nor rain these years, but according to my word" (I Kings 17:1). He was able to say this because he knew God and believed Him. "God is not a man, that he should lie; neither the son of man, that he should repent: hath he said, and shall he not do it? or hath he spoken, and shall he not make it good?" (Num. 23:19).

John the apostle fell prostrate at the feet of Jesus when he saw Him in a vision on the Isle of Pat mos. "And when I saw him, I fell at his feet as dead. And he laid his right hand upon me, saying unto me, Fear not; I am the first and the last: I am he that liveth, and was dead; and, behold, I am alive for evermore, Amen; and have the keys of hell and of death" (Rev. 1:17,18). This is our God. This is Elijah's God. This is the God of whom he said, "As the Lord God of Israel liveth" (I Kings 17:1).

Palestine experienced periods of early and latter rains, and in the interval between, heavy dews at night kept the vegetation refreshed. But there was nothing that people could do to cause rain if God withheld it. Man cannot create; that is the prerogative of God. Scientists are dabbling with seeding the clouds, but they have to have clouds before they can seed them. Only God can create clouds; people cannot do it.

One day as my wife and I were traveling we heard on the radio that in our own state of Nebraska some people had hired an old Indian chief to see if he could create rain. We began to wonder, "Are we returning to paganism in our land?" No wonder God has to speak to us today by means of hail, rain and floods. Some of them have been disastrous. God sometimes also speaks by withholding rain. Jeremiah raised this question: "Are there any among the vanities of the Gentiles that can cause rain? or can the heavens give showers? art not thou he, O Lord our God? therefore we will wait upon thee: for thou hast made all these things" (Jer. 14:22).

I gather from the record that at the time Elijah faced Ahab with the news of God's judgment, the drought had existed for six months. This lack of rain was the result of the direct prayer of Elijah who based it on God's statements recorded in

15

Deuteronomy. The prophet had not gone to see Ahab immediately but had waited until Ahab and the nation were in dire need of rain. Then he told Ahab that there would be no dew or rain—not only for months but for years until he, Elijah, gave the word.

Elijah was in a place of danger when he stood before Ahab. The evil woman the king had married sought the life of every servant of God that she could find.

God's prophet had no prestigious position or wealth that might have made Ahab hesitant about destroying him. Elijah was a rough mountaineer dressed in a garment made from camel's hair, a poor man whose life Ahab might take without any qualms of conscience. Yet the prophet stood before the king and claimed the six-month drought was due to his intercession before God.

How could a man who had no standing socially or governmentally dare to be so bold? The answer lies in I Corinthians: "For ye see your calling, brethren, how that not many wise men after the flesh, not many mighty, not many noble, are called: but God hath chosen the foolish things of the world to confound the wise; and God hath chosen the weak things of the world to confound the things which are mighty; and base things of the world, and things which are despised, hath God chosen, yea, and things which are not, to bring to nought things that are: that no flesh should glory in his presence" (1:26-29).

Elijah was a man of the same nature as we are. He was weak in himself, but he became mighty through God. These same truths apply to us today. We, too, can be bold in situations when we know we are in the will of God. We may be unknown and have nothing that the world would highly regard, such as family, social position or education; but since it is God who supplies the power, we can accomplish His tasks. We learn from II Corinthians 10 that "though we walk in the flesh, we do not war after the flesh: (for the weapons of our warfare are not carnal, but mighty through God to the pulling down of strong holds;) casting down imaginations, and every high thing that exalteth itself against the knowledge of God, and bringing into captivity every thought to the obedience of Christ" (vv. 3-5).

The Secret of Elijah's Strength

We, too, can do God's work in God's power if we will take time as Elijah did to speak before God in the secret place and then go out by faith in the zeal and energy of the Lord. The first part of his secret was his prayer life.

We must never lose sight of James 5:17,18: "Elias was a man subject to like passions as we are, and he prayed earnestly that it might not rain: and it rained not on the earth by the space of three years and six months. And he prayed again, and the heaven gave rain, and the earth brought forth her fruit."

This is the means that God uses with His people. We learn in Ephesians 6:18 that we are to pray with all supplication in the Spirit. Praying in the Spirit means to be prompted by the Spirit in what we pray for. In Elijah's case, God had decided that it was time for the people of Israel to be reminded of what He had told them through Moses. God said that if they would obey, they would be blessed; but if they disobeyed, they would be chastised. God needed a man to pray that this judgment would be put into effect. He found such a man in Elijah. The prophet prayed earnestly, and God shut up the heavens so that it did not rain.

Elijah was unafraid when he stood before Ahab because he had knelt in humility before Almighty God. The Lord gives grace to the humble, but He resists the proud. For this reason we are to submit ourselves to God, but we are to resist the Evil One, and he will flee from us. "Draw nigh to God, and he will draw nigh to you. Cleanse your hands, ye sinners; and purify your hearts, ye double minded" is the admonition we're given in James 4:8. Having obeyed this admonition, we can pray and we will receive. When we are right with God in our hearts, then we will ask for the things that please Him, and He will answer us.

Elijah had a knowledge of God. This was another reason for his strength. He not only knew the names of God and His mighty works, but he had a personal inner knowledge of Him. It was the kind of knowledge of which Paul spoke in Philippians 3:10: "That I may know him, and the power of his

17

resurrection." Ahab did not worship God, but Elijah did. God was a living reality to Elijah. He should be to us also.

Many people today have a very low view of God. They do not understand who He is or what He wants to do or how able He is to do all He plans. Such people lack purpose in life. Unless they come to know Him through Jesus Christ, they will end up lost and without hope. They will be utter failures. In contrast to these people are the ones spoken of in Daniel 11:32: "But the people that do know their God shall be strong, and do exploits." God is looking for such persons according to II Chronicles 16:9: "For the eyes of the Lord run to and fro throughout the whole earth, to shew himself strong in the behalf of them whose heart is perfect toward him."

Do you know the Lord in this way? Do you know Him intimately? This is how Elijah knew Him, and this was one reason why God so abundantly used him.

The prophet's knowledge of God was a growing knowledge. He spent time at the Brook Cherith and learned to know God intimately. He then spent time in Zarephath where God wonderfully supplied his needs in the home of a poor widow. There again Elijah grew to know God better. This was God's program for Elijah until He called him home to be with Himself.

Paul also taught us that our knowledge of God should always be increasing. After stating, "That I may know him, and the power of his resurrection" (Phil. 3:10), Paul wrote: "Not as though I had already attained, either were already perfect: but I follow after, if that I may apprehend that for which also I am apprehended of Christ Jesus. Brethren, I count not myself to have apprehended: but this one thing I do, forgetting those things which are behind, and reaching forth unto those things which are before, I press toward the mark for the prize of the high calling of God in Christ Jesus" (vv. 12-14). Let us also press on, for then we will be strong in the power of His might.

Another reason for Elijah's strength was his knowledge of God's presence. God was not someone whom he had met on some previous occasion, perhaps in Gilead, perhaps in some mountain hideaway. Instead, He was the Lord God of Israel "before whom I stand," Elijah said (I Kings 17:1). The prophet recognized he was always in the presence of God. The knowledge of this truth has a remarkable effect upon a person's thinking and actions and character.

We who belong to the Lord are always in His presence. He has promised, "I will never leave thee, nor forsake thee" (Heb. 13:5). We do not see Him with our physical eyes, and we may even be unaware of His presence, but He is with us.

Elijah knew that even while he stood in the presence of King Ahab, he was also standing in the presence of One who was infinitely greater. Since Almighty God was with him, why should he tremble before a mere human king?

Our Lord said we were to go out into the whole world, and He added this promise: "Lo, I am with you alway, even unto the end of the world" (Matt. 28:20). He sends us out, but He goes with us. This is good to remember when we are tempted to be discouraged or when we feel that God has stopped answering our prayers. We may not feel His presence; the great essential is to know His presence. Our feelings are only fleeting emotions. They easily come and go, but knowing is based on the Word of God, and that Word is true. Elijah was a strong man of God and a bold witness because he was conscious of God's presence all the time.

A fourth factor with regard to his unique ministry was that he gave out the unchanging Word of God in a constantly changing world. The world does change quickly, but does it change us with it? Do we tend to give in to the world's spirit, compromising our standards in order to be less objectionable to worldly people? It is a sad fact that many Christians have grown careless in this area of life.

Are the things of the world occupying our attention so much that we neglect our responsibilities to our Lord? Does the television take up our prayer time? Do we follow the world's ideas more closely than we do the standards God has set in His Word?

God has never changed, but people do. With regard to the subject of divorce, for example, someone may ask, "Are you still holding to the old-fashioned doctrine that there should be no divorce? Everybody thinks differently today." It is true that this is not a popular position. Remember, however, that people differed with our Lord Jesus Christ on this very question. He brought them back to first principles when He reminded them that in the beginning it was not so (Matt. 19:3-12). The Lord has not changed, and so why should we?

Because the ideas of the world are changing, because its educational systems are changing, because its philosophies are changing, and because Western civilization is going back to heathenism in many ways, should Christians follow along and do likewise? Shouldn't we rather be willing to stand alone if necessary for the truth of the Word of God? In this way we will show that we are true children of God and that Christianity has genuine standards.

Elijah was the man he was because he was a man of faith. Remove the element of faith from him even for a moment, and you will find him to be weak, fearful, discouraged and wishing to die. This was his experience after the great victory at Mount Carmel, He was threatened by Jezebel, and he fled for his life. Instead of keeping his eyes on God, he wanted to give up. But God was faithful to him, and in His unchangeable goodness He encouraged and sustained His servant.

The God whom Elijah worshiped is my God. He has not changed in the centuries since Elijah's day. The God who stopped the rain from falling on Palestine for three and one-half years is my God. The God who sent the rain when He decided it was the right time is my God. The God who sent fire from heaven to consume Elijah's offering on Mount Carmel is my God. He is the same God today as then.

This means that if we believe God and are obedient, we, too, will be effective in our service. The power of the Holy Spirit will be given so we can do what God wants us to do according to the measure of our faith. Power belongs to God, and we can be strong in the power of His might.

Paul learned that he could do all things through Christ who strengthened him. The apostle found that his weaknesses could be made strong when he trusted God. Faith must be tested and matured, and God will lead us along as far as we are willing to go with Him. Elijah, being a man like us, had his weak moments, but he faced the trials of faith and became triumphant.

Chapter 3

Elijah at Cherith

One of the basic points concerning driving an automobile at night is that one should never over drive the distance that the headlights shine. If the lights shine 100 yards ahead of the car and the driver can see that far, he should be sure to drive at such a speed that he would be able to safely stop within that distance. There is a basic lesson for us in this with regard to the Christian life, a lesson that shines clearly from the experience of Elijah. We are not to go farther than God plans for us. We are not to go ahead of Him but to travel one step at a time.

The prophet said when he stood before Ahab, "As the Lord God of Israel liveth, before whom I stand, there shall not be dew nor rain these years, but according to my word. And the word of the Lord came unto him, saying, Get thee hence, and turn thee eastward, and hide thyself by the brook Cherith, that is before Jordan. And it shall be, that thou shalt drink of the brook; and I have commanded the ravens to feed thee there" (I Kings 17:1-4). As we have previously seen, Israel had been experiencing a drought for at least six months. Thus, it was dangerous for Elijah to stand in the presence of Ahab and tell him who was responsible for the lack of rain. Elijah was not ignorant of the dangers, knowing that Jezebel had killed all the prophets of God she could reach, but he obeyed God. He came before the monarch and gave him God's message. This was as far as Elijah was told to go, but as soon as he had obeyed, God had additional instructions for him.

One Step at a Time

Obeying God always comes first, then He reveals the next step. Too many of us, in doing the work of God, want to see the end result immediately. But that is not trusting God, that is trusting sight. Faith does not see; it trusts and obeys. When Elijah had delivered His message to Ahab, the Lord told him what his next step was to be. Tradition says that this brook ran into the Jordan about 15 miles above Jericho. Its waters came from the mountains of Ephraim from a spring concealed under a high cliff and shaded by a dense jungle. It is probable that it was in such a spot that God hid His servant — a place of safety made known after Elijah's first step of obedience.

As we are obedient and search the Scriptures, God will show us the next step we are to take in our spiritual lives. This is always God's way of working. When Saul was on his way to Damascus, he suddenly saw a great light. He realized that he was face to face with the Lord and said, "Lord, what wilt thou have me to do?" (Acts 9:6). The Lord replied, "Go on to Damascus, and there you will be told what you should do" (see v. 6). Saul had to take a step of obedience. He waited three days, and then the answer came.

When Joshua led the people of Israel into the land, God assured him: "Every place that the sole of your foot shall tread upon, that have I given unto you" (Josh. 1:3). This is what we call the law of appropriation. Every step Joshua took claimed more of the land for him and the Israelites. God was not going to give the Israelites the land all at once. They had to appropriate it one step at a time. It was at the moment the priests entered the Jordan River that it parted. It was as the Israelites completed their walking around the city of Jericho that the walls collapsed. In obedience to God they went forward step by step, and then God gave them what they needed.

The same was true concerning the manna. It was provided every morning, six days a week. However, it was provided just one day at a time. In the Lord's prayer we are taught to say, "Give us this day our daily bread" (Matt. 6:11). What strength or encouragement we need will be given us, for God has said,

"As thy days, so shall thy strength be" (Deut. 33:25). Let us remember that the Lord's work is done one step at a time.

God Asks Our Absolute Trust

We learn also from Elijah's experience that the servant of God must trust Him absolutely. God told Elijah to go to the Brook Cherith and stay, for He had commanded the ravens to feed him there. At no other place would the ravens feed Elijah but at the Brook Cherith, at the spot designated by God. This raises some questions: Are we where God wants us? Are our troubles the result of our being out of the will of God? We will always face troubles in this world, but this should not discourage us. God provides grace to help us. Some troubles, however, are caused by our not being where God wants us. Such troubles are remedied only as we obey God.

The ravens were to bring Elijah his food at Cherith. Suppose, however, he had thought he knew a better hiding place and had gone to some spot in the mountains of Gilead? He could have starved to death, for the ravens had not been commanded to go there. The ravens were told by God to go to the Brook Cherith, by those high cliffs near the Jordan River where a special stream was fed by a spring. There God would protect Elijah from Ahab. The brook bordered the land of Samaria, the very land over which Ahab was king. There God protected His servant.

When the Israelites were passing through the wilderness, the manna fell wherever the pillar of cloud or the pillar of fire led them. The needed water was always found when the people followed the guiding hand of God.

The great principle covering this is stated in the New Testament in these words: "Seek ye first the kingdom of God, and his righteousness; and all these things shall be added unto you" (Matt. 6:33). Let us seek to be in His place of service, doing His will, doing His work in His way, and He will take care of our needs. "Trust in the Lord with all thine heart; and lean not unto thine own understanding. In all thy ways acknowledge him, and he shall direct thy paths" (Prov. 3:5,6).

Faith Tested

As Elijah stayed by the brook, the ravens brought him bread and meat in the morning and bread and meat in the evening, and he drank of the waters of the stream (see I Kings 17:6). But a time of testing arose, for the brook dried up. It, too, was affected by the lack of rain. Elijah began to experience the results of his own prayer. He undoubtedly had known what would happen when he prayed as he did, but he probably did not know exactly when the water would stop flowing.

Why would God test him like this after having directed him to go to this brook? Why didn't God keep the water running in a miraculous way if necessary? An incident in the Gospel of John furnishes us with a very possible answer. "When Jesus then lifted up his eyes, and saw a great company come unto him, he saith unto Philip, Whence shall we buy bread, that these may eat? And this he said to prove [try] him: for he himself knew what he would do" (John 6:5,6). God knew what He was going to do with His prophet, and it was all for his spiritual well-being. We can picture Elijah living in that great canyon, a beautiful place covered with many trees. Little by little the water in the brook began to recede; after a while the birds and animals left the area, for they no longer had water to drink. Elijah probably had to dig a hole in the sand to collect a little water for his personal use.

No doubt he wondered if God would forget him. The tempter, the Devil, is never far away from those who are seeking to do the will of God; he might have tried to upset Elijah. Perhaps he tempted Elijah to become discouraged with doing the will of God, or he might have suggested that Elijah go back home because he had sinned and was reaping God's displeasure. Satan might even have encouraged him to formulate his own plans and to take matters into his own hands, then to ask God to bless those plans.

In Isaiah 28:16 we are told, "He that believeth shall not make haste." Apparently Elijah knew this truth and obeyed it. When things seemingly go wrong, we should wait on God and not be in a hurry.

We are admonished in Hebrews 13:5,6: "Let your conversation be without covetousness; and be content with such things as ye have: for he hath said, I will never leave thee, nor forsake thee. So that we may boldly say, The Lord is my helper, and I will not fear what man shall do unto me."

Why did God allow the brook to dry up? One reason may have been to teach Elijah, and us, not to trust in the gifts that God gives but always to trust in God Himself. This is very important. We must keep our eyes on God, not on things, not on gifts, not on blessings. There is a strong tendency today for some believers to have an experience in the Holy Spirit and then to get their eyes off the Lord and on that experience, on the gift instead of the Giver.

It must have been hard for Elijah to sit by the brook and watch it disappear, but God was teaching him to turn his eyes from the failing stream to the unfailing God. Then just when the brook dried up completely, the word of the Lord came to him again and told him where to go.

Unbelief looks at the circumstances, forgetting God's power. For example, the ten Israelite spies who returned with a negative report had seen only the great walls and giants in the land of Canaan (see Num. 13). They concluded that they could not take the land.

But faith looks at the circumstances through God. Goliath was a giant, but when David looked at God and saw how powerful He was, Goliath looked very small (see I Sam. 17:31-58). So when faith looks at God instead of at the circumstances, the circumstances take on their proper proportion.

Another reason why God tested Elijah's faith at Cherith was that His servant needed this private schooling in order to meet further situations. He was already noted for his zeal and for the effectiveness of his prayer life. He had asked God that rain be withheld from Israel, and God had answered his prayer. Since Elijah was like us, he might have become proud. He could easily have begun to gloat over his success in prayer. The Lord knew this whether Elijah did or not, and He knew that Elijah needed further schooling.

The Apostle Paul had a similar experience that he described in II Corinthians: "And lest I should be exalted above measure through the abundance of the revelations, there was given to me a thorn in the flesh, the messenger of Satan to buffet me, lest I should be exalted above measure. For this thing I besought the Lord thrice, that it might depart from me. And he said unto me, My grace is sufficient for thee: for my strength is made perfect in weakness. Most gladly therefore will I rather glory in my infirmities, that the power of Christ may rest upon me. Therefore I take pleasure in infirmities, in reproaches, in necessities, in persecutions, in distresses for Christ's sake: for when I am weak, then am I strong" (12:7-10).

The man whom the Lord uses to perform certain tasks must be humble. The self-life can rise to the surface very quickly, and we must all beware of it. God will not share His glory with anyone, though in due course, He will honor those who have been faithful to Him.

Before God could use Elijah further, He had to train him. So I believe that his seclusion was intended to provide more than protection from Ahab's vengeance.

Many examples of this are found in Scripture. Joseph, the son of Jacob, was sold as a slave to Egypt but soon rose to be the most trusted servant in Potiphar's household. God, however, had a larger task for this young Israelite, and in order to prepare him for it, he was placed in jail for a crime he did not commit and was seemingly forgotten. Nevertheless, God was training him for greater things. At the right time Joseph was released from prison to become the prime minister of Egypt and the preserver of his own people.

Moses became a great man as the son of Pharaoh's daughter. He was in a position to become ruler of Egypt by reason of his adoption into the royal family. He renounced this position, however, and identified himself with his own people, a nation of slaves. He presented himself to the Israelites as their deliverer, but he was not ready for the task. God taught him for 40 years in a desert region and, when he was ready, brought him to be the great emancipator and leader of Israel.

The same truth is seen in the life of David. He showed great promise even while he was a young man, both as a soldier and as a man who wanted to do the will of God. He first came to Israel's attention when he killed Goliath. Yet, after this great success and some others that followed, God allowed him to be persecuted and tested in order to make him the man He wanted him to be.

If God is going to use any of us, He will have to seclude us in some way so that He can personally make us what He desires us to be. When we stay where God wants us and do as He directs, He obligates Himself to fully sustain us. We need to learn to stay where God puts us until He moves us. It is easy for us to let circumstances move us out of the will of God. Perhaps we are having difficulties making ends meet, or we feel that we are not receiving the income that we should receive for our work. So, we start planning and perhaps scheming to change our way of life and our locality if necessary in order to get the material things we want. We reason that if we are in the will of God, He will not allow us to suffer financial reverses and that a test in this realm is a clear indication that we should move. This could be true but not always. It was not so in Elijah's case. He stayed by the brook and saw it was gradually drying up; but since God had placed him there, he was not going to move until God told him to.

Think also of the instruments God uses at times. God used ravens to preserve Elijah's life. To the Israelite these were unclean birds. They were not to be used as food. The tendency was to avoid them. Nevertheless, God used them, thus showing His absolute sovereignty in His choice of instruments. God does not always choose the person who seemingly has all the potential for great service. God, in His sovereign purpose, chooses whom He will to do His work.

By feeding Elijah through ravens, God showed His supreme power. He did what He had promised. These birds brought food day after day to Elijah, even when the brook was drying up. They were under God's direction and never once failed in their appointed task.

Here is what the psalmist said in this connection: "What-soever the Lord pleased, that did he in heaven, and in earth, in the seas, and all deep places" (Ps. 135:6). All nature obeys Him. Do we? Nature has no free will, but we do. We ought to be the ones who willingly obey Him since it is our privilege to fellowship with Him. The lower creatures in nature do not have such a privilege; nevertheless, God uses them to perform His will.

In carrying out His purposes, God uses both the natural and the supernatural. In Elijah's case, the brook was a natural means of satisfying the prophet's need for water. At the same time, since Elijah had prayed that God would withhold the rains and the dew from Israel, the brook began to dry up. This was a natural consequence of God's answer to his prayer. On the other hand, the fact that the ravens brought the prophet his food day after day was supernatural. They were not doing what was normal and usual to their nature. Their feeding of Elijah was a daily miracle.

When the Children of Israel escaped from Egypt and traveled to Canaan, God performed many miracles. He gave them manna from heaven, the flesh of birds and water from rocks. As for their clothing and shoes, these did not wear out while the Israelites lived in the desert. God has His own ways of doing things since He is sovereign. When God calls us to do something for Him, it is not our business to inquire how He is going to do it. Our responsibility is to obey. It is God's business to choose the method He will use.

It is conceivable that Satan might have tempted Elijah to think that the ravens would eat the food themselves and not bring it to him. There is no record that this took place, but if Elijah had thought such a thing, he would have been putting his faith in the instrument instead of in God. His faith, however, was in the Lord and not in the instrument. We, too, must place our trust in the Creator and not the creature.

The promise of Philippians 4:19 is that God will supply all our needs according to His riches in glory by Christ Jesus. There is no point in our trying to find out how God will do this. Our responsibility is to believe that He will.

Chapter 4

Elijah at Zarephath

Because Elijah was a man like us, he undoubtedly wondered what God had in store for him when he saw the brook beginning to dry up. Since he was trusting in God, however, he believed and help arrived. God did not send a sudden squall of rain for that immediate neighborhood, nor did he provide some supernatural source of water in that place. Instead, "The word of the Lord came unto him, saying, Arise, get thee to Zarephath, which belongeth to Zidon, and dwell there: behold, I have commanded a widow woman there to sustain thee" (I Kings 17:8,9). Elijah was to arise, go to Zarephath and dwell there. Only at Zarephath would a widow provide food for him.

Elijah was sent to the country from which Jezebel came, a heathen country where most of the inhabitants worshiped Baal. The journey was long and hard, for Zarephath was about 100 miles from Cherith. Elijah had to travel on foot through many wild and barren places during a great famine. Added to this was the danger of passing through the country over which Ahab ruled. Nevertheless, Elijah obeyed.

The word Zarephath means "refining" or "smelting place." This land was ruled by Jezebel's father who was a heathen tyrant and a wicked idolater like his daughter. God's purpose in sending Elijah there was to use it in his life as a smelting furnace that would remove the dross of pride or any tendency to self-reliance or independent action apart from Him. The Lord was preparing a clean vessel for the next great step in His plan of deliverance and cleansing for Israel.

Elijah arose and went to Zarephath, "and when he came to the gate of the city, behold, the widow woman was there gathering of sticks: and he called to her, and said, Fetch me, I pray thee, a little water in a vessel, that I may drink" (v. 10). We are not told how many days Elijah traveled, but when he arrived at the city, he found the person he was looking for. God often works in more than one way to make all of the details fall into place when we obey Him. He never leaves any detail untouched.

In verse 9 this woman was simply designated "a widow woman." Her name was not given nor were any other details. Whether she was rich or poor, a Jewess or a Gentile was not told him. In verse 10 the words are "the widow woman." The definite article indicates that this was the woman God had in mind. She was the only widow who had been commanded of God to provide for His servant.

We can see this, of course, since we have the Bible, for it makes it plain that this was the woman God had in mind. Elijah did not know this at first but tested her to see if she was the proper one. He asked her to bring him a little water in a vessel that he might drink. As she went to fetch it, he called to her, "Bring me, I pray thee, a morsel of bread in thine hand. And she said, As the Lord thy God liveth, I have not a cake, but an handful of meal in a barrel, and a little oil in a cruse: and, behold, I am gathering two sticks, that I may go in and dress it for me and my son, that we may eat it, and die" (vv. 11,12).

What a prospect faced both the prophet and the widow! She was poor to the point of being destitute. She had no resources except a handful of meal and a little oil. Yet God said, "This is the one." It must have been a humbling experience for Elijah to realize that he had been sent to the poorest of the poor in a time of famine and drought to be sustained. Should not God's prophet have the best? This is what people often say concerning the Lord's servants. In reality, Elijah did get the best, for this was God's choice for him. If the prophet had considered the circumstances only, he might have left;

but knowing that God must increase and he must decrease, he was obedient and stayed.

The Widow Tested by Elijah

Let's put ourselves in the prophet's position for a moment. He was sent to Zarephath where he was told a widow would take care of him, but he was not told which widow. Undoubtedly, there were many in that place. How was he to find the right one? He would know of the experience of Abraham's servant when he sought a wife for Isaac (see Gen. 24). The test had been whether or not the young woman would water the servant's camels without being asked to do so. It was through this that Abraham's servant found the bride for Isaac. It would seem that Elijah prayed to the Lord in very much the same way.

He put three tests to the widow. First, he requested, "Fetch me, I pray thee, a little water in a vessel, that I may drink" (I Kings 17:10). She passed this first test, but Elijah was cautious and added another. The request for water might have been answered in the affirmative by anyone, but the second request would be a different matter. He was doing God's work and seeking God's will, and he was not taking any chances; so he asked her to bring him a little bread to eat.

Her reply was one of despair and dejection. To Elijah, however, who remembered how God had sustained the Israelites in the desert and how God had just recently taken care of him at the Brook Cherith, her reply lifted his spirits. He spoke in faith when he said, "Fear not; go and do as thou hast said: but make me thereof a little cake first, and bring it unto me, and after make for thee and for thy son" (v. 13). Then he added this promise from God: "For thus saith the Lord God of Israel, The barrel of meal shall not waste, neither shall the cruse of oil fail, until the day that the Lord sendeth rain upon the earth" (v. 14).

On the surface this third test by Elijah may seem selfish. She was to bring him something before she or her son were served. Elijah's motive, however, was very apparent. He was not concerned for himself, for he knew God and knew how God could provide. Elijah was testing the woman's heart. In the words of the New Testament, he was finding out if she would seek first the kingdom of God and His righteousness and trust God to provide for her needs.

Faith acts and expects the results to follow. When God commands, we are to obey, even if what God has said is opposed to what we would expect. The circumstances did not indicate that Elijah, the widow and her son could be sustained in the midst of the famine, but God promised they would be. That was sufficient for Elijah. He knew he had found the woman who was to sustain him until the drought was over.

Faith goes ahead and trusts God for the results. The priests who carried the ark had to step into the Jordan River before the waters parted. David had to go into the field and face Goliath before he received the strength to overcome his evil foe.

People want to see the end from the beginning, but faith is content to accept what God says. There was only a little meal in the widow's barrel. But faith saw that small amount as quite sufficient because of God's promises. Elijah had first been sent to a brook where there was water but no food, and yet God supplied. Here at Zarephath there was a little something in the bottom of the barrel. Faith is not occupied with the difficulties but with the Lord with whom all things are possible. Faith is not caught up in the circumstances but is occupied with the God who controls the circumstances.

A little oil, a little meal and a little water for three persons and God — that was sufficient. Like Paul, we would declare, "How fathomless the depths of God's resources, wisdom, and knowledge! How unsearchable His decisions, and how mysterious His methods! For who has ever understood the thoughts of the Lord, or has ever been His adviser? Or who has ever advanced God anything to have Him pay him back? For from Him everything comes, through Him everything lives, and for Him everything exists. Glory to Him forever! Amen" (Rom. 11:33-36, Williams).

The Widow Tested by God

Not only did Elijah test this woman to find out if she was the person whom God had selected to provide for him, but God also tested her. He did this through Elijah, and the test showed she was obedient to God. This Gentile widow living in an environment of Baal worship obeyed the prophet's request and believed the promise of God that she would not lack food for the duration of the famine. In I Kings 17:15 we see her immediate reaction to Elijah's request: "And she went and did according to the saying of Elijah: and she, and he, and her house, did eat many days." True faith requires obedient action, a requirement that she fulfilled. As a result of her faith, her whole household, including her guest, did not lack for food.

This woman went forth in faith and did just as Elijah told her to. This obligated God to fulfill His promise. God delights to honor such faith. He wants to do it, is ready to do it and is waiting to do it for us. According to verse 16, "The barrel of meal wasted not, neither did the cruse of oil fail, according to the word of the Lord, which he spake by Elijah."

Each passing day those in this widow's household had the same test of faith—they scraped the bottom of the barrel. Yet, each day they found sufficient food in the barrel to meet their needs for that day. A consistent walk of faith requires walking with God day by day. When such a walk is sustained, God's blessings follow.

In Psalm 34:9 is a promise that has encouraged many of God's people: "O fear the Lord, ye his saints: for there is no want to them that fear him." The word "fear" in this context means "reverential fear or trust." In another psalm we learn: "No good thing will he withhold from them that walk uprightly" (84:11).

Still another promise is found in Proverbs 19:17: "He that hath pity upon the poor lendeth unto the Lord; and that which he hath given will he pay him again."

Sufficient for the Day

Few of us have faced the extremity this widow experienced. It seemed as though each day she might face starvation; yet each day by faith she trusted God to meet her need. The result was that she and her house "did eat many days" (I Kings 17:15). God supplied not a year at a time but a day at a time.

This is what we need with regard to God's grace. We do not need a great stockpile of it for future use but a daily appropriation of it, which God supplies freely. The manna was gathered daily, not in the evening but in the morning, and each one gathered for himself. So must we accept grace from God. We cannot hoard today's grace for tomorrow or call on yesterday's grace for today. We cannot appropriate enough on a Sunday to last a whole week. We need to have daily contact with God, particularly in the morning.

Paul reminded us in II Corinthians 4, "For which cause we faint not; but though our outward man perish, yet the inward man is renewed day by day" (v. 16). If we use what is given, then more will be provided. "As thy days, so shall thy strength be," we are told (Deut. 33:25). Our Saviour instructed us to pray for our daily bread (see Matt. 6:11).

Can we rejoice when our cruse of oil has only enough in it for the next day? Do we have a sense of security when the barrel of meal is not full, when there is only enough for one more day? We talk these days of material security from the cradle to the grave, and all too often our joy depends on our material prosperity. But God was teaching this widow that she could be joyful even though she only had enough oil for one day. She had this security because her eyes did not look at the barrel she would scrape each day but at the God who promised to take care of her needs.

The writer to the Hebrews gave this exhortation: "Let your conversation be without covetousness; and be content with such things as ye have: for he hath said, I will never leave thee, nor forsake thee" (13:5). God does not promise to supply everything we need for the rest of our lives right now.

If He gave it all to us now and we could see it, we would not live by faith but by sight. Faith looks to God for strength for the day, food for the day — indeed, all the needs for the day. The life of faith is a step-by-step walk in conformity to the will and purposes of God.

Elijah and the widow and her son would look to God and encourage themselves in His greatness. Then the widow would go to her barrel and find sufficient meal for that day. She would take what was needed, believing that, because of God's greatness and power, there would be sufficient meal in the barrel again the following day. The same was true with the oil.

The Spirit and Power of Elijah

A significant statement is made concerning Elijah in Luke 1: "For he shall be great in the sight of the Lord, and shall drink neither wine nor strong drink; and he shall be filled with the Holy Ghost, even from his mother's womb. And many of the children of Israel shall he turn to the Lord their God. And he [John the Baptist] shall go before him [Jesus] in the spirit and power of Elias [Elijah], to turn the hearts of the fathers to the children, and the disobedient to the wisdom of the just; to make ready a people prepared for the Lord" (vv. 15-17).

For the Scriptures to say that John the Baptist was to go before the Lord "in the spirit and power of Elias" is a testimony to the fact that Elijah was a man of spiritual power. James told us he was a man of the same nature as we are; yet he was a man full of the Holy Spirit. In the Old Testament economy, for the Holy Spirit to indwell and control a man as Elijah was indwelt and controlled, was something special. But in this age, it is the privilege of every born-again believer to be indwelt by the Holy Spirit. In Old Testament times God picked out certain men for specific purposes and empowered them with the Holy Spirit to carry out those purposes. In this age, as the Apostle Paul told us, the believer's body is the temple of the Holy Spirit. We are not our own. We are the temple of God, and the Spirit of God dwells in us (I Cor. 6:19,20).

This indwelling of the Spirit is in response to our Lord's prayer recorded in John 14:16,17: "And I will pray the Father, and he shall give you another Comforter, that he may abide with you for ever; even the Spirit of truth; whom the world cannot receive, because it seeth him not, neither knoweth him: but ye know him; for he dwelleth with you, and shall be in you."

Elijah was responsible to God in a very special way since he was filled with the Spirit of God for a particular work. We not only have the indwelling of the Spirit, but we can be filled, or controlled, by the Spirit in order to fulfill the purpose of God in our lives. He will hold us accountable for how well we have fulfilled His purpose at the Judgment Seat of Christ according to II Corinthians 5. We will be rewarded for what we have done that pleases God and will lose rewards for what displeases God.

In writing to the Ephesians Paul declared, "In whom ye also trusted, after that ye heard the word of truth, the gospel of your salvation: in whom also after that ye believed, ye were sealed with that holy Spirit of promise" (Eph. 1:13,14). The apostle did not say that we were sealed "by" the Holy Spirit, which would make the Holy Spirit the instrument of our sealing. Rather, he said we were sealed "with" the Holy Spirit, which means that the Holy Spirit is our seal. He is the "earnest of our inheritance" (v. 14). He has been given to us until the "redemption of the purchased possession" (v. 14). The moment we became children of God, the Holy Spirit took up His residence in us. But in order for us to be filled with the Holy Spirit, we must give Him possession of every aspect of our lives. He must control every phase of our being.

From the life of Elijah we learn that there are three simple conditions for being controlled by the Holy Spirit.

Empty of Self

First of all, we must be empty of self. God cannot fill us if we are already filled with the self-life. Elijah was emptied of self during that long period of three and one-half years of drought and waiting on God. His experiences first at the

Brook Cherith and later at Zarephath taught him that he could do nothing of himself. He could not even provide food for himself. Even water, one of the most common commodities of life, was available to him only through God's provision.

It was in proportion to his being emptied of self and self-sufficiency and self-dependence that he was filled with the Holy Spirit of power. So, while Elijah waited on the time when God would deal in this very specific way with Israel, the Holy Spirit was taking more and more possession of him. Later, of course, there was the great triumph at Mount Carmel, but that triumph was not possible until God had full possession of His servant.

Some people seek more of the Holy Spirit, but this is wrong. They have this matter turned around. The Holy Spirit is seeking more of us. He already indwells each believer. For us to have His fullness does not mean that we should seek more of Him but that He should be given control of all areas of our lives.

Some people look within themselves for evidence of His indwelling and refuse to believe in His presence unless they can detect some sign of His presence. This is also wrong. The Scriptures make it plain that we are indwelt by the Spirit the moment we receive Christ as our Saviour. We accept this by faith. He will take complete control of our lives as we fulfill the three conditions seen in Elijah's experience.

In one of His great discourses our Lord said, "If any man thirst, let him come unto me, and drink. . . . This spake he of the Spirit" (John 7:37,39). If we thirst for the filling of the Holy Spirit, then Christ will fill us. We do not drink when we are already full — only when we are thirsty. We drink when we have a need. We must recognize the emptiness of self before we can drink of His fullness. The Lord's promise is "He that believeth on me, as the scripture hath said, out of his belly [innermost being] shall flow rivers of living water" (v. 38).

The evidence, then, of the Spirit's presence in us does not lie in signs but is accepted on the basis of faith. I accept what God says, and that settles it. The Holy Spirit does not make Himself known to us by signs pointing to Himself, for

He reveals not Himself but Christ: "Howbeit when he, the Spirit of truth, is come, he will guide you into all truth: for he shall not speak of himself; but whatsoever he shall hear, that shall he speak: and he will shew you things to come. He shall glorify me: for he shall receive of mine, and shall shew it unto you" (16:13,14).

One of the surest indications of the presence of the indwelling Spirit is sensitiveness to sin. It is a sad commentary on professing believers that many of them talk about the fullness of the Holy Spirit in their lives; yet they evidence cantankerousness and argumentativeness, which are works of the flesh and not fruit of the Spirit. Tenderness of conscience is another evidence of the Spirit's presence. We will also find Christ increasingly precious and will be in sympathy with His purposes in the world and in our own hearts.

Obedience

The second condition for the fullness of the Holy Spirit is obedience. When God told Elijah he must go to a certain place, he went. Some of the conditions may have seemed extreme, but he did not question them. He did as God said. For example, it was an exceedingly dangerous step for Elijah to enter the presence of Ahab. Yet, God told him to go, and Elijah went.

It was rather an odd thing for God to tell him to hide at the Brook Cherith and he would find food and water there, but this he did also. Then, when the brook dried up, God told him to go to Zarephath where he would find a widow who would sustain him. Elijah obeyed and found God's promises to be fulfilled to the letter. Later, when God decided it was time to send rain, He told him to show himself to Ahab the second time. Elijah did this without hesitating. The point is that he was obedient to whatever God told him to do.

We are filled with the Holy Spirit only as we continue in obedience. The Holy Spirit's fullness is given only for the fulfilling of God's purposes. We must be subject to His directions and plans without reservation.

The Word, Our Spiritual Food

The third condition is that we must realize that the Word of God is our spiritual food. The Holy Spirit works through the Word of God. Only as we feed on it day by day do we meet God's conditions.

Our Saviour said in John 6, "As the living Father hath sent me, and I live by the Father: so he that eateth me, even he shall live by me. This is that bread which came down from heaven: not as your fathers did eat manna, and are dead: he that eateth of this bread shall live for ever" (vv. 57,58). A little later in the chapter He explained that eating His flesh meant obeying His Word. He said, "It is the spirit that quickeneth; the flesh profiteth nothing: the words that I speak unto you, they are spirit, and they are life" (v. 63). So the third condition for being filled with the Spirit is to let the Word of God rule in our hearts.

A neglected Bible means that we will be starved and strengthless spiritually. Many people run to meetings for spiritual help, but they do not meditate on the Word of God for themselves. Let us learn to go to the Word for our counsel.

We meet the conditions of the filling of the Spirit when we are emptied of self, are obedient to what God directs and feed constantly on the Word of God. This is the way to power. Let us follow the admonition of the psalmist, who said, "But his delight is in the law of the Lord; and in his law doth he meditate day and night. And he shall be like a tree planted by the rivers of water, that bringeth forth his fruit in his season; his leaf also shall not wither; and whatsoever he doeth shall prosper" (Ps. 1:2,3).

Elijah's Private Life Put to the Test

Can God do for us what He did for Elijah? Was He just the God of Elijah, or is Elijah's God our God? These are not idle questions but go to the very heart of the significance of these Scripture passages we have been studying.

Elijah was thoroughly tested in both his public and private life. Sometimes we can make impressions as believers in public that are much better than our conduct in private. How do we react when the toast is burned or the steak is overcooked? How do we respond when cherished plans are altered by circumstances? Perhaps someone comes to us for help or a family condition arises that needs attention—how do we respond to these needs? People who are filled with the Holy Spirit will be the same in public and in private. The Spirit-controlled person exhibits the fruit of the Spirit anywhere he happens to be.

First Kings 17:17,18 says, "And it came to pass after these things, that the son of the woman, the mistress of the house, fell sick; and his sickness was so sore, that there was no breath left in him. And she said unto Elijah, What have I to do with thee, O thou man of God? art thou come unto me to call my sin to remembrance, and to slay my son?" We can think of extenuating circumstances for this mother who was bereft of her son. She had possibly been tending him night and day as he lay on his sickbed, and her nerves were strained to the breaking point. She spoke unadvisedly and cruelly to this good man who had brought to her home nothing but kindness and the blessings of God.

Elijah might have been trapped into giving a quick and sharp answer. After all, he was innocent of the accusation she made. However, in spite of the provocation, he did not lose his poise.

The death of her son apparently reminded the widow of some past sin. Her conscience was aroused, and she wanted to vindicate her character in her own eyes. Under such circumstances a person wants to turn the blame, if there is any, on someone else.

We realize that she very likely had a heathen background and had been a worshiper of Baal. It is possible that by this time she believed in the true God, but the death of her son was a great shock to her. Her conscience for some reason or other was aroused, and our conscience can make us very uncomfortable.

Without a doubt Elijah's holy life had convicted her of sin. This can happen to any of us. Sometimes this conviction comes from a member of our own family — a child perhaps or a wife and mother whose good life makes others in the home aware of their evil ways. Joseph's brothers were convicted of their past mistreatment of him when they encountered trouble in Egypt.

When we encounter problems in our life, it is difficult for us to understand the reason for them. Perhaps our reaction to some sorrow or loss or problem is "Do I deserve this?" or "Why has God treated me so harshly?" If we have lost a loved one, perhaps we asked why God took that loved one. We wonder why we have to suffer and why our neighbors do not. This is the carnal nature expressing itself, not the spiritual nature.

See how Elijah met this difficult situation: "And he said unto her, Give me thy son. And he took him out of her bosom, and carried him up into a loft, where he abode, and laid him upon his own bed" (v. 19). What a gentle answer Elijah gave! He had been falsely accused by someone who was not a stranger, for he had been dwelling in the home of the widow for quite some time. It is true they did not have an abundance of food, but they were not starving. They had little variety, but they were eating twice a day at least and had water to drink. The fruit of the Spirit was seen in Elijah's response — love, joy, peace, long-suffering, gentleness, goodness, faith, meekness and self-control. Elijah was the same kind of man privately that he was publicly.

Love, according to I Corinthians 13, "suffereth long" (v. 4). It is kind, it is not easily provoked, and it bears all things and endures all things. Perhaps some will say Elijah could react this way because he was specially filled with the Spirit of God. That is true, but he had the same old nature we have, and he had to contend with it at all times. It was not eradicated, but he did not have to obey it, for it was crucified with Christ. Paul said, "I am crucified with Christ: nevertheless I live; yet not I, but Christ liveth in me: and the life which I now live in the flesh I live by the faith of the Son of God, who loved me, and gave himself for me" (Gal. 2:20). The Holy Spirit is the only Person who could produce this kind of fruit in a life.

We are no different from Elijah in this respect. The same Spirit who indwells us indwelt Elijah and can do for us what He did for him. Elijah responded to the Spirit's dealing in his life and gave himself over completely to Him. Elijah knew that if God was to use him to the fullest extent, he would have to walk close with Him.

A habit that has blessed my own life is that when I am through working in my study, located in the basement of my home, I pause before leaving it and ask myself this question: "Am I ready to go out in service?" I review my spiritual condition and ask myself if I am going out in His name. Many times I have said, "Lord, I will not go unless You bless me in a special way. I cannot go unless You touch me with Your Spirit in a very definite way. I want to fulfill Your business in a way that is right and say things in a spirit and power in which You want them said. I cannot go without the consciousness of Your presence." I have then left my study assured that God would use me.

Elijah had spent much time in the presence of the Lord; so the death of this young lad and the unfair accusation by his distraught mother did not affect his spiritual poise. He took the boy in his arms and prayed, "O Lord my God, hast thou also brought evil upon the widow with whom I sojourn, by slaying her son?" (I Kings 17:20). The Lord had sent him to that widow's home, and she had graciously taken care of him for many months, possibly a year or more by then. Elijah wondered why God had permitted this to happen. Then, we are told: "He stretched himself upon the child three times, and cried unto the Lord, and said, O Lord my God, I pray thee, let this child's soul come into him again" (v. 21).

It is clear that Elijah fully believed that God would answer his prayer. He did not pray in a public gathering, for some matters are best discussed with God alone. Some things are accomplished only as we wrestle privately in prayer.

Elijah showed perseverance. He did not give up but stretched himself upon the child three times. We are inclined to give up too soon. We ask God once or perhaps twice, and then, because we receive no answer, we stop asking. The

Lord Jesus admonished us to be persistent in our praying. When we're praying in God's will, we should keep on asking.

As we stop to consider this matter a little more, we realize that Elijah was asking for something that had not been previously recorded in all human history. There is no record of God's having raised anyone from the dead from the time of Adam to the time Elijah prayed for the widow's son. Perhaps he caught the truth from Abraham's prayer concerning Isaac, for Abraham most certainly believed in the God of the resurrection. But whatever the source, Elijah was asking for something new in human experience. But he could ask this because he knew God. Ephesians 3:20 says, "Now unto him that is able to do exceeding abundantly above all that we ask or think, according to the power that worketh in us." This was evidently Elijah's concept of God's power. So he prayed with perseverance. He prayed in faith, not wavering, for the person who wavers cannot expect his prayer to be answered.

The Word tells us that the eyes of the Lord are on the righteous and His ears are open to their prayers (see I Pet. 3:12). In many instances the Lord is waiting for us to do some real praying. This is what Elijah did.

His one purpose in bringing this young boy back to life was to honor God. The psalmist said, "Delight thyself also in the Lord; and he shall give thee the desires of thine heart" (Ps. 37:4). God could easily give new life to this lad.

Life flowed into the boy's body again, and Elijah put him in his mother's arms. She said, "Now by this I know that thou art a man of God, and that the word of the Lord in thy mouth is truth" (I Kings 17:24). Perhaps others could say that of us if we would only trust and obey God, showing the same spirit of trust and submission that Elijah did.

Chapter 5

Elijah Approaches the Day of His Triumph

Three and a half years went by before word came to the prophet that the end of the famine was in sight. "And it came to pass after many days, that the word of the Lord came to Elijah in the third year, saying, Go, shew thyself unto Ahab; and I will send rain upon the earth. And Elijah went to shew himself unto Ahab. And there was a sore famine in Samaria" (I Kings 18:1,2). The moment of Elijah's triumph was fast approaching.

We cannot help but compare the experience of our Lord as He faced the cross with the experience of Elijah as he faced Ahab, who would gladly have taken his life. In John 17:1 we read: "These words spake Jesus, and lifted up his eyes to heaven, and said, Father, the hour is come; glorify thy Son, that thy Son also may glorify thee." Our Lord looked to the cross as His coronation day, His day of triumph and victory. Elijah was in danger of his life in approaching Ahab after three and a half years of famine.

Some years before this God had said to Elijah, "Hide thyself" (I Kings 17:3). He needed to be hidden away in order to spend time with God as well as to be protected from the vindictive Ahab. Elijah's public work needed to be laid aside for a while in order that he might be shut in with God. This was necessary so that the day of glory would be just that—a day of triumph and victory.

Elijah was a man of obedience. When God said to him, "Hide thyself" and sent him to the Brook Cherith, Elijah

45

went. He had water to drink and ravens to feed him. When the brook dried up, God said to him, "Arise, get thee to Zarephath . . . I have commanded a widow woman there to sustain thee" (v. 9). Again he obeyed and was blessed in his obedience. The third command and promise was "Go, shew thyself unto Ahab; and I will send rain upon the earth" (18:1). In each case there was a command and a promise. As the command was obeyed, the promise was fulfilled. Elijah met the condition of obedience promptly in each case.

Obedience to the instructions of God is an act of faith where the person involved commits himself entirely into the Lord's hands. It involves committing the human will and purpose into the keeping of a sovereign God. "Commit thy way unto the Lord; trust also in him; and he shall bring it to pass" (Ps. 37:5). All this is included in obedience.

No greater illustration of obedience to God is to be found than that of our Lord Himself when He said, "My meat is to do the will of him that sent me" (John 4:34). Elijah had learned the Master's secret, and that was to listen to His word. This is why it was necessary to hide himself from people. He had also learned that he must believe God, which was demonstrated by his actions. Listening to God was first, and believing Him was next. Then, when he obeyed God, the results He promised followed automatically.

Life for us is also a life of faith. Paul stated in Galatians 2:20: "I am crucified with Christ: nevertheless I live; yet not I, but Christ liveth in me: and the life which I now live in the flesh I live by the faith of the Son of God, who loved me, and gave himself for me." To the Philippians he said, "Wherefore, my beloved, as ye have always obeyed, not as in my presence only, but now much more in my absence, work out your own salvation with fear and trembling. For it is God which worketh in you both to will and to do of his good pleasure" (Phil. 2:12,13). If we will commit ourselves to the Lord completely and without reservation, He will work in us in such a way that His purposes will be fulfilled in our lives. He works in us to will and to do of His good pleasure, but He waits for our definite commitment to Him. He needs

our consent; with it His sovereign power goes into operation to carry out His purposes.

That is why Paul could say, "I can do all things through
Christ which strengtheneth me" (4:13). It was Christ in him
who caused Paul to want to do the things of God, and then, as
he consented to do those things, Christ worked through him.

Elijah had learned that in himself he was nothing. It was
possible for God to work through him only as he committed
himself to Him. He was a man of like passions as we are. God
used him because he was willing to be used by God.

Perhaps we wonder why we are not used as Elijah was.
It could be that we refuse the tests Elijah faced and passed.
When the tests come, we complain. This keeps us from learning the real secret of Christ's indwelling grace and power.
Like the Israelites in the wilderness, we complain when
we are tried. We may quote Romans 8:28,29, but we do not
believe it. That passage says, "We know that all things work
together for good to them that love God, to them who are the
called according to his purpose. For whom he did foreknow,
he also did predestinate to be conformed to the image of his
Son, that he might be the firstborn among many brethren."
God's great purpose is to conform us to the image of His Son.
If, however, we do not believe He is working in us and are not
submitting to the tests and trials that come, then we cannot
be used as Elijah was. He passed through many severe trials,
but he yielded himself to God in these experiences, and God
filled him with His Holy Spirit.

John the Baptist can teach us the secret that is involved.
He said, speaking of Christ, "He must increase, but I must
decrease" (John 3:30). Compare for a moment the Lord Jesus
to the sun and John the Baptist to the morning star. Before the
sun rises, the morning star shines clear and bright. As the day
light begins to increase, however, the light of the star begins to
disappear until it is completely out of sight. The star is still in
the heavens, but the sun outshines it so that we cannot see it.

We often speak of sanctification, but what is sanctification in the daily life? It is Christ's increasing in us and the
self-life's decreasing. Our own aims, ambitions and high

47

estimates of ourselves become less important, and Christ means more and more to us.

This was the kind of spiritual growth Elijah had experienced during those years from the time he started to pray for God to vindicate Himself before Israel until God said to him, "Go, shew thyself unto Ahab" (I Kings 18:1). Elijah was obedient because he knew his God. Had he conferred with other people, he might have been persuaded that he was like a lone swimmer plunging into a raging sea or an unarmed man walking into a lion's den. He had to present himself before a wicked, idolatrous king, a tyrant, a man armed with despotic power, whose personal enmity against God's prophet had been increasing for three and a half years.

During all this time, Ahab had sought by every means possible to find Elijah and arrest him. He had thoroughly searched his own country, as well as all the countries bordering Israel and had made those nations swear that Elijah was not among them (see v. 10). Thus, it was plain that Elijah was to face a vindictive man, but God never asks us to do what is beyond our human nature without imparting sufficient grace and strength.

In his first meeting with Ahab, Elijah had told him there would be no dew or rain until he prayed for it. Now rain was promised, for God had said it would come. It was necessary for Elijah to announce this fact, or the priests of Baal would, undoubtedly, have claimed that their god was responsible for breaking the long drought. So, in order that God's glory might be maintained and Baal completely confounded, Elijah had to be the instrument through which God would send the rain.

It is very possible that Elijah was comforted by one of David's psalms, written when danger threatened and God delivered him. "The Lord is my light and my salvation; whom shall I fear? the Lord is the strength of my life; of whom shall I be afraid? When the wicked, even mine enemies and my foes, came upon me to eat up my flesh, they stumbled and fell. Though an host should encamp against me, my heart shall not fear: though war should rise against me, in this will I be confident. . . . For in the time of trouble he shall hide me in his pavilion: in the secret of his tabernacle shall he hide me; he shall set me up upon a rock" (27:1-3,5).

Still realizing that he walked a dangerous road, David prayed, "Teach me thy way, O Lord, and lead me in a plain path, because of mine enemies. Deliver me not over unto the will of mine enemies: for false witnesses are risen up against me, and such as breathe out cruelty. I had fainted, unless I had believed to see the goodness of the Lord in the land of the living" (vv. 11-13). His final admonition was "Wait on the Lord: be of good courage, and he shall strengthen thine heart: wait, I say, on the Lord" (v. 14).

Elijah Meets Obadiah

As Elijah, in obedience to God's command, set out to meet Ahab, he saw that the famine was very severe in Samaria, one of the areas ruled by Ahab and inhabited by the Israelite people. Apparently it extended beyond Ahab's kingdom, but Samaria seemed to be getting the brunt of it. This, of course, was in line with God's judgment—He was disciplining His people. The Prophet Isaiah wrote: "If ye be willing and obedient, ye shall eat the good of the land: but if ye refuse and rebel, ye shall be devoured with the sword: for the mouth of the Lord hath spoken it" (Isa. 1:19,20). This principle was literally fulfilled before Elijah's eyes. The people had rebelled, and they were not eating of the good of the land. A large number of Israelites had probably died of starvation. The widow who took care of Elijah was on the verge of starvation when God sent him to her home for her to be the sustainer of his physical life.

Obedience to God is the key to His blessings upon us. The Israelites had suffered for three and a half years because of their disobedience, but because of the obedience of a man of God, the Lord's judgment would be lifted.

The first man Elijah met, however, was not Ahab but Obadiah, the governor of Ahab's household. "And Ahab called Obadiah, which was the governor of his house. (Now Obadiah feared the Lord greatly: for it was so, when Jezebel cut off the prophets of the Lord, that Obadiah took an hundred prophets, and hid them by fifty in a cave, and fed them with bread and water.) And Ahab said unto Obadiah, Go into the land, unto all fountains of water, and unto all brooks: peradventure we may find grass to save the horses and mules alive, that we lose not all the beasts. So they divided the land between them to pass throughout it: Ahab went one way by himself, and Obadiah went another way by himself" (I Kings 18:3-6).

All that we know about Obadiah is given to us in this chapter. His life, like Elijah's, is very instructive for us. The men were not necessarily on the same spiritual level, but Obadiah was a God-fearing man who held a very influential position in Ahab's household in Samaria. He was in a position to know the terrible inroads that the worship of Baal had made in the kingdom. God had his men in high places in government before this time and after. Joseph was prime minister in Egypt, Daniel was high in the government under Nebuchadnezzar, and Nehemiah was cupbearer to Artaxerxes. Obadiah was not uncompromising like Daniel, however. Everyone knew where Daniel, Nehemiah, Ezra and some of the others stood, but Obadiah apparently was not as clear cut in his position.

God said, however, that Obadiah feared Him, even though he apparently had no influence on Ahab's spiritual life. Daniel had his enemies in court, but he also had a profound effect upon the monarchs under whom he served. Undoubtedly, Obadiah was greatly shocked when he saw Jezebel kill the prophets of God, and his conduct in preserving a number of them was highly commendable.

Obadiah evidently did not rebuke sin. He may have been like some of God's people today who say, "Don't carry this thing too far. Say just as little as is necessary to get by." Perhaps he thought his presence would influence Ahab, but it is clear that he did not get very far. He did not live the life of a separated man who stood for the truth of God as some of the others did. He was satisfied with being defensive concerning his faith, but he was not aggressive in witnessing. He did not actively promote the cause of God.

God used him and recorded no criticism of him. God simply painted the picture so that we could see what kind of person Obadiah was. However, it is clear from II Corinthians 6:14,15 what the believer's position should be in the midst of idolatry and unbelief: "Be ye not unequally yoked together with unbelievers: for what fellowship hath righteousness with unrighteousness? and what communion hath light with darkness? And what concord hath Christ with Belial? or what part hath he that believeth with an infidel?"

Then the admonition is given for the believer to be separate: "Wherefore come out from among them, and be ye separate, saith the Lord, and touch not the unclean thing; and I will receive you, and will be a Father unto you, and ye shall be my sons and daughters, saith the Lord Almighty. Having therefore these promises, dearly beloved, let us cleanse ourselves from all filthiness of the flesh and spirit, perfecting holiness in the fear of God" (6:17 – 7:1). Believers today need to obey this principle.

We find in II Timothy 2:21 another principle: "If a man therefore purge himself from these, he shall be a vessel unto honour, sanctified, and meet for the master's use, and prepared unto every good work." Obadiah had done some good things, but his compromising left him unprepared to be used as fully as God would like to have used him.

Elijah stood in contrast to all this. He was not a great man as the world would measure greatness. He was not the prime minister of a powerful nation, nor did he hold the position that Obadiah held in the house of Ahab. Elijah belonged in the category that Paul described in I Corinthians 1:26-29. Here we are told that God did not choose many mighty nor many wise; instead, He called mostly the weak and the despised to do His work. He chose some great men, such as Daniel and Paul, but usually He calls ordinary people.

Obadiah held a position of prestige and influence in overseeing Ahab's household and possessions. But instead of Obadiah's lifting up Ahab, apparently Ahab tended to drag Obadiah down so that he was more concerned about herds and possessions than about the will of God.

Does this speak to our hearts? Perhaps God allowed this man's life to be included in the Scriptures to teach us this lesson.

Ahab and Obadiah had divided the land between them in their search for pasture for the animals, and while Obadiah was searching, Elijah met him. He greeted the prophet with these words: "Art thou that my lord Elijah?" (I Kings 18:7).

Obadiah's Fear

Elijah commissioned Obadiah to tell Ahab that he was looking for him. Obadiah's response was one of fear. He said, "What have I sinned, that thou wouldest deliver thy servant into the hand of Ahab, to slay me?" (I Kings 18:9). This man seems to have lacked moral strength and spiritual backbone. When the commission was given, he was reluctant to obey. He was afraid that Elijah would vanish before he could return with Ahab and that Ahab would then slay him. But Obadiah finally accepted Elijah's commission and carried the message to his master.

Fear proved disastrous to Peter when he was walking on the water. He did well until he took his eyes off the Lord and looked at the waves. So it was with Obadiah, who looked at the circumstances around him instead of trusting God.

Obadiah may have recognized the possibilities of God's power but, like many of us, did not see it as something for himself. The great things God could do were for somebody else, not for him. Before he agreed to tell Ahab that he had met Elijah, he had to be assured that Elijah would stay where Ahab could find him. Obadiah did not want Ahab's wrath to fall on him. This is why he said, "And it shall come to pass, as soon as I am gone from thee, that the Spirit of the Lord shall carry thee whither I know not; and so when I come and tell Ahab, and he cannot find thee, he shall slay me" (v. 12).

Then Obadiah went on to vindicate himself in Elijah's eyes: "But I thy servant fear the Lord from my youth. Was it not told my lord what I did when Jezebel slew the prophets of the Lord, how I hid an hundred men of the Lord's prophets by fifty in a cave, and fed them with bread and water?" (vv. 12,13). Obadiah did here what many of us are doing today, namely pointing to statistics as proof of our faithfulness to God. Obadiah gave the number of the prophets he had helped; yet while he was doing it, he was afraid to be Elijah's messenger to Ahab.

The similarities between Obadiah and Elijah are few, and the contrasts are many. They were both God-fearing men, and both had a commission. Elijah had a commission to show himself to Ahab, and Obadiah had a commission to tell Ahab that Elijah was coming. But this is about as far as their similarities went.

Contrasts Between Elijah and Obadiah

These two men contrasted greatly with regard to obedience. When God told Elijah to do something, he did it without hesitation. Obadiah, on the other hand, hesitated, fearing for his life. He lacked faith in the power of God. Elijah never questioned for a moment that God would provide the power needed for his commission. Obadiah believed God had such power, but he did not believe it was for him personally.

Elijah was a man of great courage; boldness marked his life. Obadiah was the opposite; he was a man of fear.

Elijah did not worry about his reputation. When he was on Mount Carmel, he staked his whole reputation on his belief that God would answer by fire. Obadiah was distressed as soon as he heard Elijah commission him, and he became defensive, trying to build up his own reputation by telling what he had done at a previous time.

Elijah had a positive message. He asked his nation why they hesitated between two opinions (see I Kings 18:21). He knew that whoever was not for God was against Him. Obadiah did good things, such as feeding the Lord's prophets, but apparently he was not convicted of his sins of omission.

As for results, Elijah prevailed on God to act. At Mount Carmel fire fell from heaven, demonstrating the faithfulness of God. Rain came as God had promised. But as for Obadiah, he was a spectator of these things. Without a doubt he was glad to see God vindicated and rejoiced that Baal had been discredited, but he personally had no part in the results. Let us not overlook the fact that we, too, can rejoice that God is working through others. But why not have the joy Elijah had by watching God work through us? Elijah was human, just as we are, and it is God's desire to accomplish His purposes through His children.

Elijah was recognized as one of God's greatest men. He was even taken to heaven without dying, and some say that he is to return to prepare the world for Christ's return. He was a man whom God could depend on. As far as Obadiah is concerned, this particular man is not heard of again in Scripture.

Why not check our own lives against the lives of these two men. Where do we stand? Are we where God wants us? Is God able to use us, or are we rejoicing only in what He is doing through others? Let us learn to know Him. Let us take time to do so, for this knowledge does not come overnight. Time spent in the presence of God brings eternal results.

A View of Ahab's Character

We have already seen Ahab to be an infidel, a blasphemer, even though he was king of the ten tribes of Israel. As far as his homelife was concerned, he might be described as a "henpecked husband." It is apparent that his strong-minded wife, Jezebel, ran his life. We have already seen that she imposed her religion on her husband and on his kingdom.

Ahab gave the following instructions to Obadiah: "Go into the land, unto all fountains of water, and unto all brooks: peradventure we may find grass to save the horses and mules alive, that we lose not all the beasts. So they divided the land between them to pass throughout it: Ahab went one way by himself, and Obadiah went another way by himself" (I Kings 18:5,6).

While Elijah was on his way to see Ahab, the king had also set out on a journey. Elijah was on an errand for the honor of God, the God of Israel. Ahab was searching for food for his horses and mules. He had no concern about God. The country had seen three and a half years of famine, and Ahab knew that his sin and that of his household and Israel's apostasy had brought this drought upon his kingdom. But he still had no concern for his own sin and no thought of repentance toward God. Relief from divine judgment was all that he thought about or cared about; he made no attempt to remedy the situation that had brought the judgment. He was very much like Pharaoh, who, when a plague struck, called for Moses and asked Moses to pray to have the plague removed. Then, once the judgment had been removed, Pharaoh returned to his former evil ways.

This is characteristic of unregenerate men. We read in Revelation 16: "And the fifth angel poured out his vial upon the seat of the beast; and his kingdom was full of darkness; and they gnawed their tongues for pain, and blasphemed the God of heaven because of their pains and their sores, and repented not of their deeds" (vv. 10,11).

One would think that Ahab, as king of Israel, would have been more concerned about his people than about his animals. Such was not the case, however. By shutting God out of first place, Ahab's evil heart seemed incapable of rising any higher than being concerned for his horses and mules.

How different this was from David, a man after the heart of God. When he saw that the judgment of God was about to fall on Israel because of his own personal sin, he pleaded that his people might be spared and that he might be punished, for he, not they, did the evil (II Sam. 24:17).

We are living in days of danger and judgment. We pray for revival, but why? Is it in order that the character of the days might change? Do we want God to restrain the evil forces for His glory or for our comfort? Elijah wanted to see God honored before the whole nation, but Ahab sought only relief from the results of the drought.

Ahab was so infuriated against the prophet of God that he had sought him everywhere. Instead of looking at his own evil deeds, Ahab had considered Elijah to be the cause of all his trouble and the worst enemy of his nation. Ahab wanted to destroy him, but he first had to find him. He could not locate Elijah anywhere in Samaria, and his search throughout the neighboring countries ended with the same result. Elijah was not to be found.

Elijah's Boldness

It was with God-given boldness that Elijah met this merciless and despotic ruler. He was willing to give his life for the honor and glory of God.

At a later time, Paul the apostle, when warned that if he went to Jerusalem he would have nothing but trouble, gave this answer: "But none of these things move me, neither count I my life dear unto myself, so that I might finish my course with joy, and the ministry, which I have received of the Lord Jesus, to testify the gospel of the grace of God" (Acts 20:24). Paul had one task to fulfill, and he was determined to do it.

At another place, when he was warned again of what was before him, Paul answered: "What mean ye to weep and to break mine heart? for I am ready not to be bound only, but also to die at Jerusalem for the name of the Lord Jesus" (21:13). Surely things would begin to happen if we had this kind of love and devotion to Christ! This was the attitude that characterized Elijah. He was God's servant and cared only about the mind and will of God. Elijah was God's bondslave, and a slave does not originate his own plans.

How do we fit in to this type of wholehearted devotion to the Lord? Is our eagerness only for the success of our work or our church? If these thrive, are we satisfied? If these do not thrive, do we become depressed?

When a person is satisfied that he is in the center of God's plan and that God is working out His will through him, that person is invincible. Other people and circumstances, whether they mean opposition or even death, are of no importance to us. Fulfilling the purposes of God is what counts to such a person.

Like Paul, this person will be obedient to the heavenly vision. He will also believe that no circumstances can exist without God's permission. Paul's attitude was this: "If God wants me to die in this thing, then I am ready to die." This was also Elijah's attitude.

Even weak Samson, in his last moments before his death, prayed for God's strength that he might serve Him just once more. He recognized that he had played the fool, but he wanted only one more opportunity, and God gave it to him. Samson killed more Philistines then than in all of his previous experience. But it cost him his life to do it (see Judg. 16:23-31).

Elijah had been alone with God. He had been tested and trained and taught. He knew his God and was ready for whatever Ahab might try to do. The monarch's first words were "Art thou he that troubleth Israel?" (I Kings 18:17). I am not sure how Ahab said that, but I have a feeling he was shaking in his boots. He was standing before a man who had been in the presence of God. Though Ahab could say to his servants, "You do this and do that" and though he was sur-rounded by his bodyguards, I am sure he was awed in the presence of Elijah.

The king's accusation was false, and under such circum-stances the normal reaction is for a person to justify himself. A Spirit-filled person, on the other hand, has surrendered all his rights and has no self to justify. Elijah might have mod-erated the king's displeasure by telling him that rain was on the way, but that was not the message Ahab needed at that moment. The king and his people had to be humbled before God. God's glory was at stake, and His honor had to be vin-dicated. Thus, Elijah's answer was fearless. He sought no favor from the king.

Elijah Charges Ahab

Even though Ahab's bodyguards were with him and would have slain Elijah at the king's command, the prophet minced no words. These soldiers held no terror for him. The language he used is seldom heard in our day to rebuke leaders of nations who are doing wrong. "I have not troubled Israel; but thou, and thy father's house, in that ye have forsaken the commandments of the Lord, and thou hast followed Baalim" (I Kings 18:18).

57

People are usually quick to flatter and to seek their own praise. This could have happened to Elijah as he stood before Ahab, but it did not. Elijah had been in God's school of training and had been hidden away with God for three and a half years. There Elijah had learned how to stand in the name of God before others, regardless of who they might be.

Another tendency is for us to deal with sin in a general way. To name the sin and denounce the sinner as Elijah did is quite bold. He said to Ahab very much what Nathan said to David: "Thou art the man" (II Sam. 12:7).

Paul, in writing to Timothy, gave us further insight into speaking the truth: "I charge thee therefore before God, and the Lord Jesus Christ, who shall judge the quick and the dead at his appearing and his kingdom; preach the word; be instant in season, out of season; reprove, rebuke, exhort with all longsuffering and doctrine. For the time will come when they will not endure sound doctrine; but after their own lusts shall they heap to themselves teachers, having itching ears; and they shall turn away their ears from the truth, and shall be turned unto fables. But watch thou in all things, endure afflictions, do the work of an evangelist, make full proof of thy ministry" (II Tim. 4:1-5).

Like our Lord Himself, we are not to speak of ourselves but to speak what the Father gives us. As ambassadors for Christ we are to beseech others to be reconciled to God (see II Cor. 5:20). We are "vessels" whom God fills with His life, His courage, His grace, His power and His strength.

Elijah's charge against Ahab and his household was that they had departed from God and had rejected His Word. Any group or nation that does this ends up in trouble as Ahab and Israel did. Ahab would not allow God to rule over him nor his house nor his people. This is the attitude of many people in churches today.

But is it not also the attitude of many of us who would not verbally deny the lordship of Jesus Christ? We may not reject His rulership in so many words, but our actions show we reject it. Our lack of surrender indicates it. Our failure to give our life to Him unreservedly is proof that we are not allowing Him to rule over us. We do not refuse Him as personal Saviour, but we refuse Him the place of Lord and Master. We want the good things of life, but if He touches our lives or property or finances or maybe calls our children for His service, then, like the Christ-rejectors of old, we say, "No, we don't want this man to rule over us" (see Luke 19:14).

This story of Elijah and Ahab is history and was written for our benefit. We must apply it to our own hearts if we are to be helped by it.

Elijah, as the representative of God, issued orders to Ahab. The prophet commanded and the king complied. This was an unusual situation. Here was a man without a government position. The king looked on him as a mortal enemy. He had prayed that it would not rain, and it did not rain, and because of that Ahab wanted to arrest and kill him. Yet he had the audacity to say to Ahab, "Send, and gather to me all Israel unto mount Carmel, and the prophets of Baal four hundred and fifty, and the prophets of the groves four hundred, which eat at Jezebel's table" (I Kings 18:19).

God, by signs and wonders and mighty deeds, was going to overthrow Baal in one day. This is not stated at this point, but this is what God was leading up to in directing these events. Apostasy has to be judged, and God, who is longsuffering, must eventually bring whatever judgment is needed to correct the wrong situation.

The world will witness just such a judgment when the Lord brings down His wrath on those who deny that the Lord Jesus Christ is the eternal God come in the flesh and impose their own ideas on others. In Revelation 17 and 18 we learn that the world church will be brought to an end very quickly. "Her plagues come in one day, death, and mourning, and famine; and she shall be utterly burned with fire: for strong is the Lord God who judgeth her" (18:8).

A little later the Scriptures say, "Alas, alas, that great city Babylon, that mighty city! for in one hour is thy judgment come. . . . For in one hour so great riches is come to nought. . . . For in one hour she is made desolate" (vv. 10,17,19).

In light of such departure from the living God, believers can do only one thing with regard to such a church organization. God's instructions are "Come out of her, my people, that ye be not partakers of her sins, and that ye receive not of her plagues. For her sins have reached unto heaven, and God hath remembered her iniquities. Reward her even as she rewarded you, and double unto her double according to her works: in the cup which she hath filled fill to her double" (vv. 4-6).

It was because he was a man of faith that Elijah spoke so boldly and courageously to Ahab. We are told in Hebrews 11:33,34: "Who through faith . . . out of weakness were made strong, waxed valiant in fight, turned to flight the armies of the aliens." This is what faith will do. The judgment on the prophets of Baal and their religion was ordained of God; Elijah was the man He had selected to be His representative.

Elijah's weapons were not carnal. They were the same weapons we have for our warfare: "Weapons . . . mighty through God to the pulling down of strong holds; casting down imaginations, and every high thing that exalteth itself against the knowledge of God, and bringing into captivity every thought to the obedience of Christ" (II Cor. 10:4,5). This is what takes place when faith claims God's promises and acts in obedience.

Ahab dared not disobey. Though he had been raging throughout the country for years, seeking Elijah's life, when Elijah stood before him, he was afraid. The king saw that Elijah was a man of God and that the power of God was with him: so Ahab sent for the people of Israel and gathered the prophets of Baal together with them on Mount Carmel.

The king was made a coward by his sins. His conscience accused him. At a later time in history, Herod, when he heard about Jesus, thought it was John the Baptist come back to life. When Paul stood as a prisoner before Felix, it was Felix who trembled. Paul was in chains, but he reached the conscience of the ruler before him. Mary, Queen of Scots, feared John Knox's prayers more than she feared the armies of England. Evil people may put on a false front before God's messenger, but inwardly they tremble, for the truth of God pierces their heart.

Chapter 6

The Hour of God's Triumph

An altar to Baal had been erected on Mount Carmel. Long before that, however, one had been erected to the Lord, but for many years it had been in ruins. The place chosen was prominent and accessible. It was not some hidden, out-of-the-way area. People look for such places when they want to hide their sins: "Everyone that doeth evil hateth the light, neither cometh to the light, lest his deeds should be reproved" (John 3:20). God chose Carmel to expose the sin of Israel and to demonstrate His own power and glory.

Ahab complied with Elijah's orders to gather Israel and the prophets of Baal at Mount Carmel. He had no other choice. Unless Elijah gave the word, there would be no rain, and the famine would continue. So, in spite of all of his threats against Elijah's life, King Ahab was obedient to the prophet's commands and did what was required. This was also a demonstration of the power of God over the hearts of men: "The king's heart is in the hand of the Lord, as the rivers of water: he turneth it whithersoever he will" (Prov. 21:1).

The psalmist knew that God rules in the hearts and affairs of people: "Open thy mouth wide, and I will fill it. But my people would not hearken to my voice; and Israel would none of me. So I gave them up unto their own hearts' lust: and they walked in their own counsels. Oh that my people had hearkened unto me. . . . I should soon have subdued their enemies, and turned my hand against their adversaries. The haters of the Lord should have submitted themselves unto him" (Ps. 81:10-15).

61

Jehoshaphat also recognized the same truth and declared, "God, . . . art not thou God in heaven? and rulest not thou over all the kingdoms of the heathen [world]?" (II Chron. 20:6).

God worked not only in Ahab's heart but also in the hearts of the Israelites. He subdued the king so that he obeyed Elijah' s orders, and He also made the people of Israel willing to gather at Mount Carmel. Even the 450 prophets of Baal attended, though the 400 prophets of the goddess Asherah may have anticipated what was to follow, for apparently they did not respond to the command to meet at Carmel. It is very possible that all of the Israelites, those of the king's household and the false religious leaders who came to Carmel had contempt in their hearts for Elijah; nevertheless, a power beyond themselves caused them to come.

Mount Carmel is located on the northwest corner of Palestine. It rises out of the Mediterranean Sea, and the traditional site where Elijah and the priests of Baal held their contest was about 500 feet above the sea. The highest peak of the mountain range is about 1740 feet above sea level, and a little to the southeast of it is a great plateau about 1680 feet in altitude. An altar had once been erected there to the God of Israel, but it had long since been discarded. Prominent in that place in Elijah's time was an altar to Baal. Carmel was known as "the place of the burning."

Near Mount Carmel ran the river Kishon, which never went dry in its last few miles near the sea. A precipice followed the edge of the river, and this was where the prophets of Baal were executed. Some authorities claim that these men were simply pushed over the edge and died on the sharp rocks beneath.

Southeast of Mount Carmel was the city of Jezreel. In it Ahab had another palace in which he lived on special occasions.

There must be a gap in time between verses 20 and 21 of I Kings 18. Verse 20 tells us that Ahab sent word to all the Children of Israel and gathered Baal's prophets together at Mount Carmel. This would take time. When they were gathered, "Elijah came unto all the people" (v. 21).

The gathering of this great crowd must have been a remarkable sight to behold. We can imagine Elijah's going to the highest point of the mountain and watching the people as they came by the thousands. The prophets of Baal must have made a colorful picture as they approached in their priestly garments, putting on all the pomp they could to impress the people with their dignity and power. Then the king would come with his noblemen and soldiers. Very likely there were many chariots. There would also be a great chair from which Ahab could watch the proceedings and around which the dignitaries of his kingdom would stand.

Knowing of Elijah's experience since his prayer of faith that had started the drought, he probably spent these days of waiting alone with God. He would want to know every detail of God's will with regard to the coming contest. Undoubtedly, he had looked for and found the altar of God that had been thrown down. Then there would be the problem of gathering wood and locating water. Nearby was part of a stream that never ran dry even in the dryest of seasons. Perhaps he would also find out from God where the execution of the false priests was to take place.

All eyes were upon Elijah as he came to the people. Ahab looked at him in anger and fear, the priests in contempt, the people divided in loyalty but expectant and awed by what they saw. Though Obadiah is not mentioned, he would be looking on from somewhere near the king's retinue.

Elijah was God's man who stood against the nation of Israel, its king and leaders and its false priests, but he showed no fear. He took complete control and said, "How long halt ye between two opinions? if the Lord [Jehovah] be God, follow him: but if Baal, then follow him. And the people answered him not a word" (v. 21).

Though he had a nature like ours, Elijah met this situation by faith in God and not by any inherent power in himself. Without question God's legions of angels surrounded him as he confronted this wicked king and his subjects. By faith the prophet subdued a kingdom, worked righteousness and escaped death. This is what the person whose faith is in God can do. This is what Elijah did and what we also can do when the time and the situation require it.

Elijah's Challenge to Israel

Seven times during the course of that great day, Elijah spoke, and his words were the true index of his heart. His first words were addressed to the people of Israel, not to the prophets of Baal: "How long halt ye between two opinions?" (v. 21).

Ahab and his subjects had all been trained in the knowledge of the true God. Most of them, however, including Ahab, had turned to the worship of Baal. Others were undecided. The word "halt" means "to hesitate, hobble, limp." The vast majority of them were hesitating between following Baal or following Jehovah. No doubt they dreaded the Lord because they had seen the result of the great famine in their land. Yet these same people wanted to curry the favor of the king because they were his subjects, and in order to do so they tolerated the religion of Baal.

Elijah demanded a definite decision on their part. There was only one true God, the God of Abraham, Isaac and Jacob, the great I Am. There was no other God. He will not accept a divided heart on the part of His people.

We, too, have a decision to make in this day. We must decide between the god of materialism and the God of grace. We cannot serve God and money or other material objects. The individual who is not for Christ is against Him. Joshua had to state this issue clearly to the people of Israel in his day: "And if it seem evil unto you to serve the Lord, choose you this day whom ye will serve" (Josh. 24:15). Years ago a British statesman Edmund Burke said, "The only thing necessary for the triumph of evil is for good men to do nothing."

An indictment against the Laodicean church was this: "I know thy works, that thou art neither cold nor hot: I would thou wert cold or hot. So then because thou art lukewarm, and neither cold nor hot, I will spue thee out of my mouth" (Rev. 3:15,16). The Lord Himself said this. Neutrality with regard to spiritual things is not possible. James wrote: "A double minded man is unstable in all his ways" (James 1:8).

Jonathan, the son of Saul, loved David. He knew God's plans for David and was well aware that he would one day sit on the throne of Israel. Nevertheless, Jonathan chose to stay with his father instead of joining David and his fellow outcasts. God did not allow Jonathan to live to see David on the throne. The young prince died on the battlefield with his father.

Among the religious leaders of our Lord's day were those who believed on Him: "But because of the Pharisees they did not confess him, lest they should be put out of the synagogue: for they loved the praise of men more than the praise of God" (John 12:42,43). How much better if they had followed the principle that was later stated in Hebrews 13:13: "Let us go forth therefore unto him without the camp, bearing his reproach."

Perhaps some who read this are halting between two opinions concerning salvation. Perhaps they think salvation is in the church and that by joining the church or following its rules and regulations all will be well with them. But why not listen to God instead? True salvation lies only in the Lord Jesus Christ, made possible through His shed blood. The Lord Himself clearly stated what the decision must be when He said, "Except a man be born again, he cannot see the kingdom of God" (John 3:3).

Will we, like the people of Israel, not answer a word when challenged? Theirs was the great sin of indecision already referred to in connection with the Laodiceans. They were not making a choice, and yet the Lord's word to them was "I stand at the door, and knock: if any man hear my voice, and open the door, I will come in to him, and will sup with him" (Rev. 3:20). Indecision is actually unbelief. There is no neutral ground with regard to Christ. When Elijah challenged his fellow countrymen, they answered him not a word. They feared Ahab and the priests of Baal and were not ready to commit themselves.

God was calling on His people to repent just as He did the Church of Ephesus and as He is doing today. The Lord said to that early church, "Nevertheless I have somewhat against thee, because thou hast left thy first love. Remember therefore from whence thou art fallen, and repent, and do the first works; or else I will come unto thee quickly, and will remove thy candlestick out of his place, except thou repent" (2:4,5). We must make a decision.

To the Church of Pergamos the Lord stated: "So hast thou also them that hold the doctrine of the Nicolaitanes, which thing I hate. Repent; or else I will come unto thee quickly, and will fight against them with the sword of my mouth" (vv. 15,16). These warnings are not to be lightly turned aside. It is God who speaks to our hearts and to our consciences. Let us answer Him with willing and obedient hearts.

Having thrown out a challenge, Elijah continued, "I, even I only, remain a prophet of the Lord; but Baal's prophets are four hundred and fifty men. Let them therefore give us two bullocks; and let them choose one bullock for themselves, and cut it in pieces, and lay it on wood, and put no fire under: and I will dress the other bullock, and lay it on wood, and put no fire under: and call ye on the name of your gods, and I will call on the name of the Lord [Jehovah]: and the God that answereth by fire, let him be God. And all the people answered and said, It is well spoken" (I Kings 18:22-24).

In saying that he was alone, Elijah did not mean that God was not with him. He meant that there was no other prophet to help him. The prophets of Baal were many, and he gave them first opportunity to see if their god would answer by fire.

Seeing the reasonableness of Elijah's proposal, the people assented to it at once, and this forced the prophets of Baal out into the open. They were put in the position of complying with the challenge or acknowledging that Baal was an imposter.

Yet the challenge went beyond that. It was an acid test of Elijah's faith. He gave the challenge but could not produce the result; God Himself had to provide that. The question in many minds must have been "Will God answer?" They did not have to wait long to find out.

Sowing and Reaping

According to Galatians 6:7, a person reaps whatever he sows. If he sows to the flesh, he will reap corruption, but if he sows to the Holy Spirit, he will reap everlasting life. God will not be mocked. Elijah was sowing to the Spirit and could not fail to reap of the Spirit. The prophet knew what God's answer would be.

He stood alone as a prophet of God, for though 7000 persons in Israel had not bowed their knee to Baal, they had apparently gone "underground" and were hiding, perhaps in caves or in the mountains, and had no public ministry.

It was very possible that some of these people were in the group that stood on Mount Carmel, but they did not make their presence known. Elijah stood alone; yet he was not alone, for God was with him. Someone has said that one man with God is a majority. This certainly proved to be true on Mount Carmel.

In this connection Revelation 3:8 has encouraged me again and again. Our Lord said to the Church of Philadelphia, "I know thy works: behold, I have set before thee an open door, and no man can shut it: for thou hast a little strength, and hast kept my word, and hast not denied my name." The church was small, but it honored God, and God blessed it.

Numerically the forces of unrighteousness in the world are in the majority. This was true at Mount Carmel, but the greatest power did not rest with them. Baal had thousands of followers, and apparently they were united. In fact, we have a common saying to the effect that in unity there is strength. But we must qualify that. It all depends on the kind of union. If a person is united with God in performing a work that God has determined shall be done, that one person with God can successfully stand against the whole world. A unity of large numbers of people can prove to be a weak giant because man-made unity is based on unrighteousness.

This is one reason why God often calls us to stand alone. It is then we realize that our strength lies in Him and not with the large number of followers who might have been attracted to us. Elijah with God could and did stand against the whole kingdom of Israel, even though Ahab was there with a show of force, and the prophets of Baal were there in large numbers.

God constantly seeks for a man to do His work. He said through Ezekiel, "I sought for a man among them, that should make up the hedge, and stand in the gap before me for the land, that I should not destroy it: but I found none" (Ezek. 22:30). For this reason God had to judge His sinning people.

At an earlier time in their history, God did find such a man when the nation of Israel rebelled against Him. Psalm 106:23 gives us the information: "Therefore he said that he would destroy them [Israel], had not Moses his chosen stood before him in the breach, to turn away his wrath, lest he should destroy them." In this case one man standing in the gap saved a whole nation.

Elijah was such a man in his day. He had intimate fellowship with God, and because he knew God he did great things for Him. Such a man cannot be deflected from his goal no matter what the circumstances are in his life. At a crisis time in his experience Job said, "Though he [God] slay me, yet will I trust him" (Job 13:15). A little later the same patriarch said, "For I know that my redeemer liveth, and that he shall stand at the latter day upon the earth: and though after my skin worms destroy this body, yet in my flesh shall I see God: whom I shall see for myself, and mine eyes shall behold, and not another; though my reins be consumed within me" (19:25-27). Job knew of God's intimate care for him and that He knew of his every thought. This believer of old said, "He knoweth the way that I take: when he hath tried me, I shall come forth as gold" (23:10). No wonder Job came through his trying experiences in triumph.

Because David knew God he was not afraid to face Goliath. The whole army of Israel fled in terror from the giant, but not the son of Jesse. He said to the Philistine, "Thou comest to me with a sword, and with a spear, and with a shield: but I come to thee in the name of the Lord of hosts, the God of the armies of Israel, whom thou hast defied. This day will the Lord deliver thee into mine hand; and I will smite thee, and take thine head from thee; and I will give the carcases of the host of the Philistines this day unto the fowls of the air, and to the wild beasts of the earth; that all the earth may know that there is a God in Israel. And all this assembly shall know that the Lord saveth not with sword and spear: for the battle is the Lord's and he will give you into our hands" (I Sam. 17:45-47). What faith this was!

Many Christians today shrug off these episodes of history and say that they do not apply to us. God still has a work that

He wants done, and He will give the grace, the strength and the power needed to accomplish it. "What shall we then say to these things? If [since] God be for us, who can be against us? He that spared not his own Son, but delivered him up for us all, how shall he not with him also freely give us all things?" (Rom. 8:31,32). What greater assurance do we need than this?

The God many Christians worship is too small to be the God of the Bible. We bring shame on ourselves and on our God by our lack of faith. Paul said, "I can do all things through Christ which strengtheneth me" (Phil. 4:13). And in II Corinthians 9:8 Paul declared, "God is able to make all grace abound toward you; that ye, always having all sufficiency in all things, may abound to every good work."

Ahab and all Israel knew that God had withheld rain from their land for three and one-half years. What is more, the prophets of Baal had been able to do nothing about it. Undoubtedly, they had tried but were unsuccessful.

The next test was to be a test by fire. This was within the supposed realm of the followers of Baal, for he was considered to be the lord of many aspects of nature. His devotees sometimes offered children as human sacrifices. If any god could answer by fire, surely Baal could. His prophets could not refuse this challenge without admitting they were imposters.

God has used fire on many occasions. There is little doubt that when Cain and Abel brought their offerings before the Lord, God showed His acceptance of Abel's offering by sending fire to consume it (Gen. 4:4,5).

When Abraham wanted to know how he stood with God, the Lord told him to bring an offering, and then He sent fire to pass between the parts of the sacrifice (15:17).

God said He would judge Sodom and Gomorrah and the cities of the plains. This He did by sending fire to destroy them (19:24,25).

God revealed Himself to Moses by means of the burning bush in the desert. Here again, God spoke through fire (Ex. 3:2).

In leading the people of Israel out of Egypt, through the desert and into the land of Canaan, God used a pillar of cloud by day and a pillar of fire by night (13:21). When they came to Mount Sinai and God gave them the Law, He spoke to them through thunder and lightning and an earthquake and a fire (19:16-18).

As a means of accrediting the tabernacle worship and its offerings, God sent fire from heaven to consume the burnt offering on the brazen altar. Leviticus 9:24 says, "And there came a fire out from before the Lord, and consumed upon the altar the burnt-offering and the fat: which when all the people saw, they shouted, and fell on their faces." In this case God was showing approval, but in the following chapter in Leviticus we have the record of two sons of Aaron who brought strange fire before the Lord: "And there went out fire from the Lord, and devoured them" (10:2).

When Solomon had finished building the temple and the first offerings were prepared on the altar, God showed His approval by sending fire (II Chron. 7:1).

So it was that in Elijah's day God was going to use fire to accredit His work and His servant. He would later send water, but what Israel needed first was the fire of judgment to show that the sacrifice, which was a substitute for their national sins, was accepted before God.

Summary of Fire in the Bible

We can summarize the Bible teaching concerning fire in the following way. First of all, fire is a symbol of the presence of God. This we saw when God appeared to Moses in the burning bush.

Fire is also an indication of God's acceptance of a sacrifice. On a number of occasions in the Old Testament, God showed that He was pleased with certain sacrifices by sending fire from heaven to consume them.

In the New Testament the work of the Holy Spirit is sometimes symbolized as fire (see Acts 2:3).

Fire will also be used with regard to God's judgment on unbelievers at Christ's Second Coming. For example, II Thessalonians 1:8,9 says, "In flaming fire taking vengeance on them that know not God, and that obey not the gospel of our Lord Jesus Christ: who shall be punished with ever-lasting destruction from the presence of the Lord, and from the glory of his power."

Peter also said that God will judge sinners and sin with fire: "The day of the Lord will come as a thief in the night; in the which the heavens shall pass away with a great noise, and the elements shall melt with fervent heat, the earth also and the works that are therein shall be burned up" (II Pet. 3:10).

In the last book of the Bible the awful destiny of the lost is also connected with fire: "And death and hell were cast into the lake of fire. This is the second death. And whosoever was not found written in the book of life was cast into the lake of fire" (Rev. 20:14,15).

Finally, fire is connected with God's judgment of the believer's works. We learn from Scripture, "Every man's work shall be made manifest: for the day shall declare it, because it shall be revealed by fire; and the fire shall try every man's work of what sort it is. If any man's work abide which he hath built thereupon, he shall receive a reward. If any man's work shall be burned, he shall suffer loss: but he himself shall be saved; yet so as by fire" (I Cor. 3:13-15). It is dangerous to play with fire, especially God's fire. All who play with sin or consider it unimportant are playing with fire.

Purpose of Fire on Mount Carmel

As has been pointed out before, the fire Elijah called for was to fall on the slain bullock on the altar. The slain animal symbolized the substitute for the sins of the people of Israel. If no substitute was sacrificed for the people's sins, they would have to bear the fire of God's wrath themselves. But an acceptable substitute would bear God's wrath, and the people would go free. Sin had to be judged either in the person of the sinner or in a substitute. Only Elijah's God, however, could send such fire.

For God to answer by fire was also to be an evidence of the efficacy of prayer.

71

In the third place the fire was to make clear who was the true God — Elijah's God or Baal.

Elijah had appealed to the consciences of the people when he asked them how long they would hesitate between two opinions. They did not answer him. Then he spoke to their reason when he suggested that the two bullocks be slain and placed on the two altars. The God who answered by fire would be the true God. When it was a matter of conscience, the people were quiet. But when it was a matter of seeing the wonders of God through a method that appealed to their reason, they gave their approval. They came in great numbers to watch, but their hearts stayed cold and hard. They wanted to see a miracle, but they were deaf to God's call to repentance.

The prophets of Baal chose a bullock and dressed it, but as Elijah had warned, they put no fire under it. "They took the bullock which was given them, and they dressed it, and called on the name of Baal from morning even until noon, saying, O Baal, hear us. But there was no voice, nor any that answered. And they leaped upon the altar which was made. And it came to pass at noon, that Elijah mocked them, and said, Cry aloud: for he is a god; either he is talking, or he is pursuing, or he is in a journey, or peradventure he sleepeth, and must be awaked. And they cried aloud, and cut themselves after their manner with knives and lancets, till the blood gushed out upon them. And it came to pass, when midday was past, and they prophesied until the time of the offering of the evening sacrifice, that there was neither voice, nor any to answer, nor any that regarded" (I Kings 18:26-29).

As the majority group they had been given first chance. Because there were so many of them it took them only a very short time to prepare the sacrifice. As is often the case in matters that pertain to God, however, the majority was on the wrong side.

When Elijah admonished these idolatrous priests not to put any fire under their offering, he was warning them that he would not stand for any tricks. They had often deceived people, but what they were now doing was out in the open with many eyes watching them. There was no opportunity given to these tricksters and imposters to use fire on the altar to Baal.

It is sobering to realize that at the Great White Throne Judgment there will be no opportunity for tricks or deceit on the part of those charged with sin and rejection of Christ. Everything will be in the open. Numbers 32:23 will be completely fulfilled: "Be sure your sin will find you out."

It was not beyond the power of Satan to have sent fire and to have thus deceived the people with regard to Baal and his prophets. With God's permission the Evil One was allowed to send fire that burned up Job's sheep and servants (Job 1:16). According to Revelation 13 the beast out of the earth will make the inhabitants of the earth worship the Antichrist and will do great wonders, one of which will be to make fire come down from heaven (v. 13). But in this open trial between Satan and God on Mount Carmel no fire fell for the false priests. No false religion can put away sin by sending fire to consume the vicarious sacrifice. No false religion can bestow the Holy Spirit. The prophets of Baal were doomed to failure.

Baal's Frenzied Priests

Dr. Alfred Edersheim in his *Old Testament Bible History* gives the following account of this scene based on authentic information: "Now commenced a scene which baffles description. Ancient writers have left us accounts of the great Baal-festivals, and they closely agree with the narrative of the Bible, only furnishing further details. First rose a comparatively moderate, though already wild, cry to Baal; followed by a dance around the altar, beginning with a swinging motion to and fro. The howl then became louder and louder, and the dance more frantic. They whirled round and round, ran wildly through each other's ranks, always keeping up a circular motion, the head low bent, so that their long dishevelled hair swept the ground.

"Ordinarily the madness now became infectious, and the onlookers joined in the frenzied dance. But Elijah knew how to prevent this. It was noon — and for hours they had kept up their wild rites. With cutting taunts and bitter irony Elijah now reminded them that, since Baal was Elohim, the fault must lie with them. He might be otherwise engaged, and they must cry louder.

"Stung to madness, they became more frantic than before, and what we know as the second and third acts in these feasts ensued. The wild howl passed into piercing demoniacal yells. In their madness the priests bit their arms and cut themselves with the two-edged swords which they carried and with lances. As blood began to flow the frenzy reached its highest pitch, when first one, then others, commenced to "prophesy," moaned and groaned, then burst into rhapsodic cries, accusing themselves, or speaking to Baal, or uttering incoherent broken sentences. All the while they beat themselves with heavy scourges, loaded or armed with sharp points, and cut themselves with swords and lances — sometimes even mutilated themselves — since the blood of the priests was supposed to be specially propitiatory with Baal" (Vol. VI, pp. 17,18).

The frenzy of Baal's prophets reached its height at noon. In the excitement generated by the rhythm and speed of the priests' action, it would not have taken a great deal for the people watching them to have been swept off their feet emotionally and to have joined in the wild orgy. But Elijah was ready for this very thing. He very effectively used the weapon of sarcasm to expose the intentions of these evil men and at the same time to insure emotional stability among the observers.

We read in Psalm 2:4 that God will laugh and hold in derision the plots of those who rebel against His government. Something like this happened when Elijah spoke as he did. God was using a human instrument and a human life but with supernatural power back of it. These men were fools, and God was answering them according to their folly.

We can see God's attitude again in Proverbs 1: "Because I have called, and ye refused; I have stretched out my hand, and no man regarded; but ye have set at nought all my counsel, and would none of my reproof: I also will laugh at your calamity; I will mock when your fear cometh; when your fear cometh as desolation, and your destruction cometh as a whirlwind; when distress and anguish cometh upon you. Then shall they call upon me, but I will not answer; they shall seek me early, but they shall not find me: for that they hated knowledge, and did not choose the fear of the Lord: they would none of my counsel: they despised all my reproof. Therefore shall they eat of the fruit of their own way, and be filled with their own devices" (vv. 24-31).

It is possible that Israel had never seen such earnestness and enthusiasm at any previous time. But such things are no proof that the cause is good and true. Some people assume that such a display of zeal and fervor is evidence of spirituality; however, this can be far from the truth.

Elijah Prepares the Sacrifice

Probably about three hours passed, and it was time to call off the futile efforts of the idolatrous priests.

Elijah called the people of Israel to come near him, and he repaired the altar that had been broken down. This was the time of the evening sacrifice, and final preparations were made for God to answer by fire.

The people were invited to come close because he wanted them to witness every move. Elijah wanted them to see that no trickery was involved in what he was doing. Truth does not fear the closest investigation. It does not shun the light; in fact, it invites it. The broken altar was a silent witness of the broken fellowship between the people and their God. It first had to be repaired. Before God could remove the judgment of the drought, their sin had to be taken care of.

The principle on which God was working appears in II Chronicles 7:12-15: "And the Lord appeared to Solomon by night, and said unto him, I have heard thy prayer, and have chosen this place to myself for an house of sacrifice. If I shut up heaven that there be no rain, or if I command the locusts to devour the land, or if I send pestilence among my people; if my people, which are called by my name, shall humble themselves, and pray, and seek my face, and turn from their wicked ways; then will I hear from heaven, and will forgive their sin, and will heal their land. Now mine eyes shall be open, and mine ears attent unto the prayer that is made in this place."

Israel's broken altar should remind us of the danger of our altars being broken down. What is our relationship with God? Is it kept intact daily? Or is there a lack of repentance in our hearts? God's instruction to Israel in the passages quoted from II Chronicles is also His recipe for a revival in a Christian's heart.

Before any of us can do anything for the Lord we must be in right relationship with Him. Then we must seek to arouse our fellow Christians to do the same thing. After succeeding here we can reach out to lost souls. Unfortunately, many of us turn these things around. We preach to the lost but overlook the need of our own relationship and fellowship with God. We must first get right with Him before we can do an adequate job of pointing others to Him. And if we have unconfessed sin in our life and we do not repent of it, we block our own approach to God. "He that covereth his sins shall not prosper: but whoso confesseth and forsaketh them shall have mercy" (Prov. 28:13). The psalmist said, "If I regard iniquity in my heart, the Lord will not hear me" (Ps. 66:18).

The Lord had to remind the Church of Ephesus that they had left their first love and unless they returned He would have to remove the church. Abraham went to Egypt during a lapse of faith, and it was only after he came back to the altar that he had a new beginning and fresh promises from God.

It is very significant that though Elijah was dealing with the Northern Kingdom during the time of the division of Israel, he used 12 stones, thus signifying Israel's oneness and unity. It was not God's will for them to be a divided people.

Once the altar was repaired, Elijah dug a trench around it and had water poured on the sacrifice and the wood until the trench was full.

The Altar

There are lessons to be learned from the significance of the altar. The altar itself spoke of prayer and surrender. The trench around the altar stood for complete separation from any man-made rituals. God's truth has its source in God and not in men. The woman at the well asked our Lord where worship should be conducted—in Jerusalem in the temple or on the mountain set apart by the Samaritans for that purpose. Our Lord told her that a time was coming when the true worshipers of God would worship Him in spirit and in truth without the need of any special place designated for it (see John 4:23). True worship is not created by man. We gather in our churches, and the services should be conducive to worship. But though the emotional atmosphere may make people think they are worshiping, it may not be true worship at all.

Wood was laid on the altar and was necessary for the burning of the sacrifice. The wood spoke of the cross and pointed forward to the crucifixion of our Lord. Finally, there was the sacrifice itself on which the fire was to fall. For the fire to fall was not enough; it had to fall on the proper object. Fellowship between God and His people could be restored only when the proper sacrifice was accepted by Him through fire.

We could never have a proper relationship with God without Christ's substitutionary death for us on Calvary. He was the sacrifice offered on our behalf. Only through Him can we approach God. Had He not died, we would be alienated from God today.

The part the water played in this sacrifice was unique. The fact that it was poured over the bullock and the wood and filled the whole trench insured that no ordinary power would be able to consume the sacrifice. It almost appeared that Elijah was making it hard for God to answer. But nothing is too hard for God. It is possible that this water was obtained at a nearby spring that never ran dry. It has been suggested, however, that the people who had come at Elijah's command may have brought their own water. It was a very precious commodity since it was so scarce during the drought. They

77

may have been induced to pour their own water on the altar. If they did, their action would speak to us of sacrificing things that we consider precious.

God calls on us to present to Him the most precious thing we have. Paul wrote about this in Romans 12:1: "I beseech you therefore, brethren, by the mercies of God, that ye present your bodies a living sacrifice, holy, acceptable unto God, which is your reasonable service."

Some may think that their body is not the most precious thing in the world to them, but for most people it is. Satan asked God for permission to afflict Job and then said, "Skin for skin, yea, all that a man hath will he give for his life. But put forth thine hand now, and touch his bone and his flesh, and he will curse thee to thy face" (Job 2:5). The Lord gave Satan permission to afflict Job's body, but He did not permit him to take Job's life. Satan went forth "from the presence of the Lord, and smote Job with sore boils from the sole of his foot unto his crown" (v. 7). Job did not react as Satan predicted, but it was not because the patriarch did not value his body.

Most of us will do anything we can to keep our bodies in the condition we would like to have them. We will spend all of our savings if need be to keep them healthy or to keep them alive as long as possible. The body is precious indeed, and that is what God wants us to bring to the altar. Of course, in yielding our body we also yield ourselves. God wants the whole person.

Elijah told the people to pour water on the altar not once but three times. They obeyed, and the whole sacrifice and altar overflowed with water. This reminds us that we may come before God and claim to have surrendered all, but the Lord may tell us to go and check everything again. When God does so, it is well for us to ask Him to examine our lives. We may be surprised at what He will reveal. As we study the Word, the Spirit works in our hearts and searches the depths of our beings. This we will have to allow Him to do over and over again. God accepts us as far as we have gone, but as we learn more truths from the Word, He reaches deeper into our hearts. He wants everything laid on the altar.

As surrendered and devoted to the Lord's cause as the Apostle Paul was, he had to admit to the Philippian believers that he had not yet attained perfection. In order to "apprehend that for which also [he was] apprehended of Christ Jesus . . . . Forgetting those things which are behind, and reaching forth unto those things which are before, [he pressed] toward the mark for the prize of the high calling of God in Christ Jesus" (Phil. 3:12,13).

The only way we can seek God's face is to have Him shine the light of His Word on us. He will show us the evil in our hearts. When we turn from the evil revealed to us, God will hear us as we pray (II Chron. 7:14).

Elijah's Prayer

By having water poured over the sacrifice as often as he did, Elijah prevented any human counterfeiting or trickery. Then he began to pray: "And it came to pass at the time of the offering of the evening sacrifice, that Elijah the prophet came near, and said, Lord God of Abraham, Isaac, and of Israel, let it be known this day that thou art God in Israel, and that I am thy servant, and that I have done all these things at thy word. Hear me, O Lord, hear me, that this people may know that thou art the Lord God, and that thou hast turned thy heart back again" (I Kings 18:36,37).

This short prayer has only 63 English words (even fewer in Hebrew), and it takes about 20 seconds to speak them. But the prophets of Baal had prayed to their idol for several hours and had received no answer at all. Elijah prayed for 20 seconds, and God answered by fire.

We will find great value in analyzing this prayer of Elijah. He addressed it to the unchangeable God, the God of Abraham, Isaac and Jacob, or Israel. This God never changes, and He is our God.

Elijah did not have some special influence with God. The prophet was a man of like passions as we are. When he addressed God, however, he sought the vindication of God's name. He said, "Let it be known this day that thou art God in Israel" (v. 36). Elijah did not pray selfishly; he sought only the honor of God.

Then Elijah asked God to make it plain to the people that he, Elijah, was God's servant. A servant, as Elijah used the word, is a person who is entirely surrendered to another. Christian service, for example, is not really something we do for Christ. It is doing the things He has assigned us to do, not what we decide to do. Furthermore, we do not do those things—Christ, who lives in us, works through us. Through our total commitment to Him, His work is accomplished in each believer.

Elijah was such a servant. He was willing to be hidden from the public. He was willing to be mysteriously fed by ravens and then by a widow for several years, willing to face the man who wanted to take his life, willing to stand in the lowest place or the highest place if only God would be honored.

On the surface, at least, the prophets of Baal did not lack devotion to their god. But in spite of their earnestness, their pleading and their frenzy, they received no answer. This was because they worshiped idols and various aspects of nature. They worshiped objects that were created by the God Elijah worshiped, the unchangeable God of Abraham, Isaac and Jacob, the God and Father of our Lord Jesus Christ.

Elijah's prayer differed in character and sincerity from that of the prophets of Baal. James described it when he said, "The effectual fervent prayer of a righteous man availeth much" (James 5:16).

Even some Christians seem to misunderstand what this verse means. They shout in prayer as though God were deaf. They put on a demonstration as though they had to attract God's attention. Earnestness in prayer does not involve physical gestures but a condition of the heart and will with regard to the purposes of God.

Perhaps here we may learn to examine our own prayers. Since Elijah's prayer was motivated by his desire to see God honored, God answered His servant. In writing concerning prayer James said, "Ye ask, and receive not, because ye ask amiss, that ye may consume it upon your lusts" (4:3). Right motives are essential if our prayers are to be answered.

The Fire Falls

It is only as we ask according to the will of God that God hears us (I John 5:14). Elijah was on Mount Carmel in the will of God, and his prayer pleased the Lord. He cried, "Hear me, O Lord, hear me, that this people may know that thou art the Lord God, and that thou hast turned their heart back again" (I Kings 18:37). Then the fire of the Lord fell and consumed the offering, the wood, the stone and the dust and licked up the water in the trench (v. 38). There was no long wait for this answer. The prophets of Baal had prayed for hours with no results. Elijah spoke this brief prayer and God answered.

God's long-suffering and mercy had already been in evidence. For years He had put up with Israel's backsliding. God is not willing for any to perish but wants all to come to repentance (see II Pet. 3:9). But He will not hold His anger against sin forever. Since He is a righteous God, He must judge, but He knows the right time to do it.

Elijah had called to the people to come near where he was standing by the altar, and they obeyed. Then the fire fell and consumed all that was on and around the altar, but none of the people were touched. The fire descended in the presence of all but directly on the altar, not on the people.

This was no ordinary fire but one that exhibited the wrath of Almighty God. It was supernatural fire that descended from God. It was not the result of spontaneous combustion or of man's work. It did not come as a result of natural law.

It first consumed the offering of the sacrifice. Pictured for us in this is the death of the substitute for man's sin. God in His righteous wrath could have consumed the people, but He consumed the sacrifice instead. This reminds us that while we were yet sinners, Christ died for us.

The offering was consumed before the wood that was intended to burn the offering. This was God demonstrating His wrath against sin and at the same time His love for sinners. The very stones of that altar were consumed by the fire. Even the dust and the water in the trench were licked up by the flames. Nothing could resist this fire from God.

So it will be when God's final judgment falls on those who have rejected the mercy provided through Christ's death. Nothing can stop that judgment when it comes. It will be a "flaming fire taking vengeance on them that know not God, and that obey not the gospel of our Lord Jesus Christ: who will be punished with everlasting destruction from the presence of the Lord and from the glory of his power" when He returns to this earth the second time (II Thess. 1:8,9).

In Revelation 20 we are given a fuller view of the judgment of the Great White Throne. All the evidence is before the divine Judge and those accused: "And whosoever was not found written in the book of life was cast into the lake of fire" (v. 15). This is what our Saviour warned of during the time of His public ministry when He told of the place where "their worm dieth not, and the fire is not quenched" (Mark 9:44,48).

Elijah acted in faith when he prayed as he did. He had God's Word on which to base his prayer. That is what made it a prayer of faith. He asked God to answer in such a way that the people would know he was God's prophet, acting according to God's Word. God could not refuse such faith; so the fire fell.

This scene at Carmel also reminds us of the statement in the Book of Hebrews that says, "Our God is a consuming fire" (12:29). God is a God of love, but He is also a God of righteousness. He cannot overlook sin. Fools mock at sin, but God cannot be mocked. If this fire had not fallen on the sacrifice prepared by Elijah, then it would have fallen upon those who had rebelled against Him. A person reaps what he sows, for God is not mocked (see Gal. 6:7). At the present God is dealing in mercy and showing long-suffering. There is a day coming, however, when He will be a consuming fire.

It is to our benefit as believers to remember that the fire of God in our lives consumes the dross of sin and self. Like a refiner of silver, God applies the heat only until the metal is pure (Zech. 13:9; Mal. 3:3).

It is no wonder that the people of Israel at Mount Carmel fell on their faces when the fire came down and said, "The Lord, he is the God; the Lord, he is the God" (I Kings 18:39).

The great controversy between Baal and God was now ended. Three and a half years of waiting for the drought to end was now over. The people had witnessed the graphic evidence of the power of Jehovah, who said of Himself, "I Am That I Am" (Ex. 3:14). They bowed before their God and Creator.

Chapter 7

Judgment and Mercy

Since God had answered Elijah's prayer by fire and the people had shown at least a surface repentance, only one more step was necessary before God could send rain. This was the removal of the prophets of Baal from Israel. They had been holding the people in spiritual bondage and were a constant threat to the future development of God's people. The step that was taken was no cruel act of savagery on the part of Elijah and those who aided him but was like the action of a people defending themselves from alien invasion. The Israelites belonged to God, and the presence among them of priests and prophets of a false religion was an invasion of God's territory.

This has its lessons for us with regard to God's attitude toward sin in our personal lives. We learn in Romans 8:13, "For if ye live after the flesh, ye shall die: but if ye through the Spirit do mortify [make to die] the deeds of the body, ye shall live." God's way of defeating the power of the flesh is to have us put to death the deeds of the body, done because we have a fallen nature.

Paul wrote to the Galatians: "They that are Christ's have crucified the flesh with the affections and lusts" (5:24). The same truth is given in Colossians: "For ye are dead, and your life is hid with Christ in God. . . . Mortify therefore your members which are upon the earth; fornication, uncleanness, inordinate affection, evil concupiscence, and covetousness, which is idolatry: for which things' sake the wrath of God cometh on the children of disobedience: in the which ye also walked some time, when ye lived in them. But now ye also put off all these; anger, wrath, malice, blasphemy, filthy communication out of your mouth. Lie not one to another, seeing that ye have put off the old man with his deeds" (3:3,5-9).

Lying, or false communication, or what other name we may wish to give it, is a serious evil in God's sight. And when it enters the realm of the spiritual, it can be extremely dangerous. Back in the Old Testament God warned Israel how they were to deal with prophets who would lead them astray from the truth. The directions are found in Deuteronomy 13:1-5: "If there arise among you a prophet, or a dreamer of dreams, and giveth thee a sign or a wonder, and the sign or the wonder come to pass, whereof he spake unto thee, saying, Let us go after other gods, which thou hast not known, and let us serve them; thou shalt not hearken unto the words of that prophet, or that dreamer of dreams: for the Lord your God proveth you, to know whether ye love the Lord your God with all your heart and with all your soul. Ye shall walk after the Lord your God, and fear him, and keep his commandments, and obey his voice, and ye shall serve him, and cleave unto him. And that prophet, or that dreamer of dreams, shall be put to death; because he hath spoken to turn you away from the Lord your God, which brought you out of the land of Egypt, and redeemed you out of the house of bondage, to thrust thee out of the way which the Lord thy God commanded thee to walk in. So shalt thou put the evil away from the midst of thee."

To have allowed the prophets of Baal to continue living and exercising all their evil practices would have exposed the Israelites to further corruption. It would have left the impression in the minds of these priests as well as the Israelites that the prophets of Baal, though agents of apostasy, were immune from judgment. God said that they were all to be destroyed. Not one of them was to escape.

Some today would charge God with being cruel for giving such instructions. We are living in an era that has rejected the Word of God and that is remarkably ignorant of His Word and His character. Most people do not know the God of Elijah.

85

They have a philosophy of coexistence with sin and advocate noninterference with sinners no matter what they do.

We as Christians are held responsible by God to put to death in our own lives the instruments of sin. We are not to destroy people but the impulses and desires in our own hearts that would lead us astray. God gives us the weapons by which this can be done — weapons that are not carnal "but mighty through God to the pulling down of strong holds" (II Cor. 10:4, see v. 5). This cannot be done through the human will but has to be done in the power of the Spirit.

We learn in Galatians 5:17, "For the flesh lusteth against the Spirit, and the Spirit against the flesh: and these are contrary the one to the other: so that ye cannot do the things that ye would." We must be unsparing in judging the evil tendencies and ways in our own lives if we are to let God control us and lead us into a closer walk with Himself. Just as none of the prophets of Baal were to be allowed to escape, so we are not to look with favor on one single sin.

In Joshua 10 we have the account of a great battle fought by Joshua against five kings of Canaan. These were defeated and hid themselves in a cave. Joshua's soldiers put rocks in front of the cave so that these men could not escape and then carried word to their leader. His answer to them was to bring out the kings and not leave them as prisoners; they were to be put to death.

Again, in Deuteronomy 17:2-5, God showed how severe Israel had to be in order to keep false teaching and evil men and women out of the land. "If there be found among you, within any of thy gates which the Lord thy God giveth thee, man or woman, that hath wrought wickedness in the sight of the Lord thy God, in transgressing his covenant, and hath gone and served other gods, and worshipped them, either the sun or moon, or any of the host of heaven, which I have not commanded; and it be told thee, and thou hast heard of it, and enquired diligently, and, behold, it be true, and the thing certain, that such abomination is wrought in Israel: then shalt thou bring forth that man or that woman, which have committed that wicked thing, unto thy gates, even that man or that woman, and shalt stone them with stones, till they die."

Whereas these were literal and physical facts in Israel's history, the spiritual lesson for us is that sin must be made inactive in our lives. The New Testament teaches us that through identification with Christ we have already died to sin (Rom. 6:1-7). So then we are to daily put into practice by faith what we have in reality under grace in salvation (vv. 11-13).

Elijah obeyed the Lord and killed the prophets of Baal. He probably took them down the steep mountainside and cast them over the precipice to the rock-filled river below. When the rains came, the bodies of the false prophets may have been washed out to sea, which was only a short distance away. This was an awful end for these men, but it signaled God's hatred for idolatry and His determination to purge His own people.

What happened in Israel is often true in our own hearts and lives as believers. We worship idols at times, because anything that takes the place of God in our lives is an idol. It can be money or homes or things.

Ahab was a witness to the death of the false prophets and may even have assented to it because of the emotional impression left by seeing the fire fall from heaven. But if this were the case, it was only temporary, for he was an apostate who, after receiving the knowledge of the truth, willfully and deliberately sinned (Heb. 10:26-29).

Elijah soon put him to the test again, and his real nature showed up. The prophet said to the monarch, "Get thee up, eat and drink; for there is a sound of abundance of rain. So Ahab went up to eat and to drink" (I Kings 18:41,42).

This was a testimony to the faith of Elijah, but it also showed once more the kind of man that Ahab was.

Before Elijah met him and instructed him concerning Mount Carmel, Ahab had been searching for pasture for his horses and mules. Apparently he had little thought for his people. Hundreds of Baal's prophets who had been fed by him and Jezebel had lost their lives, but Ahab was going back to his palace to feast. He apparently had no thought of drawing near to God and humbling himself under His mighty hand.

While Elijah went up the mountain to pray, Ahab went to eat, ignoring the fact that his land was still suffering, even though rain was promised, and that it would continue to suffer as long as a false religion was condoned and promoted by Ahab and his household.

The prophets of Baal had been judged, but Ahab had been allowed to go free. His time was coming. God is a merciful God, but He does not hold back His judgment against sin forever.

Elijah Prays for Rain

When Elijah declared that there was the sound of abundance of rain, no rain had as yet fallen. There were no clouds in the sky, no thunder and lightning, nothing that gave visible proof that rain was imminent. There was not a physical sign anywhere that rain was on the way. Elijah's statement was based on his faith in the Word of God.

Elijah knew that the Lord was the Creator and that rain was possible only as He allowed it. Undoubtedly, the prophet had read Job 28:26,27, which says, "When he made a decree for the rain, and a way for the lightning of the thunder: then did he see it, and declare it." In other words, God decided when it would rain and how much it should rain. He controlled it just as He also controls the sea into which the rivers run: "When he gave to the sea his decree, that the waters should not pass his commandment: when he appointed the foundations of the earth" (Prov. 8:29). It is the Lord "who covereth the heaven with clouds, who prepareth rain for the earth, who maketh grass to grow upon the mountains" (Ps. 147:8).

God sent judgment on the world in Noah's time through rain (Gen. 7:4,23). Through Amos the prophet, the Lord told us, "And also I have withholden the rain from you, when there were yet three months to the harvest: and I caused it to rain upon one city, and caused it not to rain upon another city: one piece was rained upon, and the piece whereupon it rained not withered" (Amos 4:7). This was why though Elijah was a man of like nature, or passions, as we are, he prayed earnestly that it might not rain, and it did not rain for three years and six months. Then he prayed again, and "the heaven gave rain, and the earth brought forth her fruit" (James 5:18). Elijah demonstrated the truth of Hebrews 11:1: "Faith is the substance of things hoped for, the evidence of things not seen." God told Elijah it was going to rain, and Elijah believed Him and acted on what God had said. That is faith.

"Elijah went up to the top of Carmel; and he cast himself down upon the earth, and put his face between his knees" (I Kings 18:42). He did not hang around to receive the congratulations of the people on the successful outcome of his contest with the prophets of Baal. He needed once more to be alone with God. While Ahab went to feast, Elijah had food, as our Saviour did, that people knew nothing of.

Those of us who preach the Gospel should follow each sermon with prayer for God's continued grace and power. Perhaps one reason why more is not accomplished through our preaching today is that we do not take time to pray after we have preached.

Elijah stood as a giant among the people at the contest on Mount Carmel. When he went higher on the mountain and came into the presence of God, he came as a poor sinner who needed mercy, and he humbled himself. In facing the forces of Baal, he was as bold as a lion. When he was alone with God, he hid his face.

Elijah had his servant with him when he went to the top of Carmel to pray, and after he had interceded he "said to his servant, Go up now, look toward the sea. And he went up, and looked, and said, There is nothing. And he said, Go again seven times" (v. 43). Seven times they went through this, and the seventh time the servant said to his master, "Behold, there ariseth a little cloud out of the sea, like a man's hand. And he [Elijah] said, Go up, say unto Ahab, Prepare thy chariot, and get thee down, that the rain stop thee not. And it came to pass in the mean while, that the heaven was black with clouds and wind, and there was a great rain. And Ahab rode, and went to Jezreel" (vv. 44,45).

Separation

There are eight different aspects of this prayer that we should consider. First of all, Elijah withdrew himself from the crowds. This called for humility on his part. The prophet did not stand before God proud and arrogant. He did not seem to express a great deal of happiness for what had happened on Carmel. He put his face between his knees as he spoke to God.

The Bible tells us to have "boldness to enter into the holiest by the blood of Jesus" (Heb. 10:19). How is this done? The same verse tells us it is done by the blood of another. We do not enter into God's presence brashly or with boasting. We do as our Lord told us to: "But thou, when thou prayest, enter into thy closet, and when thou hast shut thy door, pray to thy Father which is in secret; and thy Father which seeth in secret shall reward thee openly" (Matt. 6:6).

Elijah shut himself off from everybody else so that he could be shut in with the Lord. This is one of the hardest lessons to learn in prayer — to shut out the world and be alone with the Lord. By this we do not mean simply the physical separation into a private place but the calming of the human spirit, which is so easily upset by the turmoil of the day. "Be still, and know that I am God," the Lord has said (Ps. 46:10). The atmosphere of the world is fatal to the spirit of devotion; so it must be left behind when we enter God's presence. We must take time to rest before Him. We do not rush into His presence, pray for five minutes and then end our prayers. Real praying takes time.

Humility

In the second place Elijah's posture shows he was humble and reverent before God. Before the crowds he was majestic and dignified. As God's ambassador he pleaded with Israel. But as Israel's intercessor he pleaded with Almighty God in humility of heart and spirit.

The great victory he had just won did not cause Elijah to act flippant before God. He did not approach the Lord with a haughty spirit but was humble before Him. In Hebrews 4:16 we are told to "come boldly unto the throne of grace, that we may obtain mercy, and find grace to help in time of need." But this does not mean that we come as God's equal. It does mean that we come with confidence, knowing that when we come in the name of Christ, the Father will hear us.

Peter instructed us in these words: "Humble yourselves therefore under the mighty hand of God, that he may exalt you in due time: casting all your care upon him; for he careth for you" (I Pet. 5:6,7). James also made reference to this when he said, "But he giveth more grace. Wherefore he saith, God resisteth the proud, but giveth grace unto the humble. Submit yourselves therefore to God. Resist the devil, and he will flee from you" (James 4:6-8). Before Moses could come close to the burning bush, he had to take off his shoes because he was standing on holy ground.

Those who boldly confront and confess sin bow the lowest before Almighty God. John, who wrote the Gospel bearing his name, three short letters and the Book of the Revelation, leaned on the breast of Christ, but he expected no special favors from his Lord. When he was taken up by the Spirit into heaven and given a view of his glorified Lord, he said, "I fell at his feet as dead" (Rev. 1:17).

Confidence in God's Word

In the third place Elijah based his prayer on the promises of God. God had told him to show himself to Ahab, for He would send rain to the earth. Was it necessary for him to beg God to fulfill what He said He would do? The promises are given, not to restrain prayer but to encourage prayer. God gives us promises to show us how we should pray and to what extent we may expect an answer. These promises are the signed checks that we must endorse and present for payment.

Our Lord Himself prayed while He was on this earth. To Him the Father said in Psalm 2:8, "Ask of me, and I shall give thee the heathen for thine inheritance." The inheritance was assured to the Son, but He was told to ask for it. The promise is given, then it must be claimed, first by prayer and then by faith. This is the message of Matthew 7:7: "Ask, and it shall be given you; seek, and ye shall find; knock, and it shall be opened unto you." James reminded us that sometimes we have not because we ask not (see James 4:2). Prayer, then, is saying amen (so be it) to God's promises.

Definite

In the fourth place Elijah' s prayer was definite. He did not generalize. He was specific in what he requested. Too often we simply say "God bless" this one or that one, but we don't ask for anything specific.

Some time back I received a letter from a man who wrote concerning many interesting things, and at the close he asked me to answer him. The matters he wrote about, however, were of such a general nature that I did not know what he wanted; so I wrote to him asking what he wanted to know.

His second letter was just as general as the first. It left me as baffled as I had been before. This is often the way we approach God with regard to requests for different individuals or organizations. Let us be specific in our asking. We have been blessed "with all spiritual blessings in heavenly places in Christ" (Eph. 1:3). This is a definite promise and assurance from the Word; so let us, on this basis, ask God for special and particular things in our prayers.

Fervent

In the fifth place Elijah's prayer was fervent. He prayed earnestly. We do not need to shout and scream in order to show God that we are sincere. This is a mistake some people make. They shout as if they had to shake the walls of heaven before God could hear them.

A man (probably the preincarnate Christ) wrestled all night with Jacob, and when the Lord finally wanted to leave, His servant Jacob prayed earnestly. He said, "I will not allow you to leave me unless you bless me" (see Gen. 32:26). He was deeply sincere. It was then that God could do specific things for him.

Concerning our Saviour Himself, we read in the Book of Hebrews: "Who in the days of his flesh, when he had offered up prayers and supplications with strong crying and tears unto him that was able to save him from death, and was heard in that he feared" (5:7). This was definite, fervent praying on the part of our Lord.

Watchfulness

The sixth aspect is that Elijah prayed with watchfulness. When he asked God for rain, he sent his servant to see what was happening in the sky. The first time the servant came back and reported there was nothing; so Elijah sent him again, but he brought back the same report. The Bible instructs us to watch and pray, not to wonder and pray. Elijah had an expectant faith, and he believed God would answer. Mark 11:24 says, "Therefore I say unto you, What things soever ye desire, when ye pray, believe that ye receive them, and ye shall have them."

Perseverance

In the seventh place we find that Elijah prayed with perseverance. He prayed and then sent his servant to look. This occurred again and again. Six times the answer came back that there was nothing to be seen. When we wait patiently for the Lord, He inclines unto us and hears our cry (see Ps. 40:1). God will not break His Word. He is a God of truth, but we must wait for His time. None of us who wait on the Lord shall be ashamed (see 34:5). He grants the answer, but sometimes He waits and expects us to persevere.

Assurance

The eighth characteristic of this prayer of Elijah's was the assurance of an abundant answer. "And it came to pass at the seventh time, that he said, Behold, there ariseth a little cloud out of the sea, like a man's hand. And he said, Go up, say unto Ahab, Prepare thy chariot, and get thee down, that the rain stop thee not" (I Kings 18:44). Then the heavens became black with clouds whipped by a great wind, and the rain fell. In the meantime Ahab rode toward Jezreel.

While Elijah had been living at the home of the widow of Zarephath, a handful of meal had been all that they had seen at any time; yet it had been enough to sustain the household for many months. Consequently, a cloud the size of a man's hand was all that was needed for Elijah to know that his prayer was answered. This was why God had led him step by step through the various experiences and trials for the past three and a half years.

How we need to learn to trust God! He prepares us day by day for greater things that are coming. "All things work together for good" we read in Romans 8:28, but do we believe it?

Ahab was urged to journey swiftly to his destination, for soon the river Kishon would be overflowing, and he had to cross it while he had the chance.

The little cloud the size of a man's hand was only the first of the tremendous clouds that were to cover the sky and pour out their waters. Between the time the first small cloud appeared and the time when the heavens were completely overcast, Elijah's servant had time to get word to Ahab. A long time before, Elijah had told Ahab that it would not rain except when he, God's prophet, said it would. Now he was telling Ahab that it would rain. This, of course, was all based on the Word of God. God speaks truth. He cannot lie.

Not only did Ahab ride toward Jezreel, but Elijah ran before him to the entrance to the city. The rain poured down, and without a doubt, most of the people who were at Carmel were soon thoroughly drenched. In light of the drought conditions that had existed for so long, they would have all been thankful in spite of the fact that they were thoroughly soaked.

The scene as depicted in I Kings is remarkable. Ahab was probably still surrounded by his nobles, riding in all his pomp to Jezreel — at least 16 miles away. Then the rain began to fall, and ahead of the king ran Elijah in the power of the Lord. The countryside that had seen so much sun and so little rain was dry and hot and showed the ravages of the drought. Then suddenly the sky was filled with dark clouds, the lightning flashed, the thunder rolled, and the rain poured down. The hand of the Lord was on His prophet, and Elijah outran the chariot to the gates of the city.

Elijah girded himself for this race, which reminds us of the frequent lessons in the New Testament concerning the race we run and the need of being properly prepared for it. We are told to "lay aside every weight, and the sin which doth so easily beset us, and let us run with patience the race that is set before us, looking unto Jesus the author and finisher of our faith" (Heb. 12:1,2). We have a race to run; so let us prepare to run it in God's way.

Chapter 8

A Mighty Man Falls

The events on Mount Carmel had provided a day of triumph for God's servant. Following the miracle of the fire that fell and consumed the offering, the rain came and ended the drought in answer to Elijah's prayer. As Ahab raced toward Jezreel in the pouring rain, Elijah "ran before Ahab to the entrance" of the city (I Kings 18:46). After one of the hardest days in any man's experience, Elijah, under the power of the Lord, outran the king's chariot for at least 16 miles.

Shortly after this a reaction set in. Ahab went home and told Jezebel all that had transpired on Mount Carmel, including how Elijah had killed all the prophets of Baal with the sword. The infuriated queen then sent a message to the prophet: "So let the gods do to me, and more also, if I make not thy life as the life of one of them by to morrow about this time" (19:2).

The man who just a short time before ran before Ahab's chariot to the glory of the Lord now ran for his life. "And when he saw that, he arose, and went for his life, and came to Beer-sheba, which belongeth to Judah, and left his servant there. But he himself went a day's journey into the wilderness, and came and sat down under a juniper tree: and he requested for himself that he might die; and said, It is enough; now, O Lord, take away my life; for I am not better than my fathers" (vv. 3,4).

Elijah had been in the midst of a spiritual warfare against forces seen and unseen. The satanic powers had fought against him, but with strength provided by the Lord he had won a great victory over them. The armor of God was on him as he engaged in the battle and emerged triumphant. Then, shortly after, he suffered a spiritual downfall. How could such a thing take place, and how can we who are people of like nature escape such a fall?

Spiritual warfare must begin and be carried on in humility. Paul's words come to us with new force: "Finally, my brethren, be strong in the Lord, and in the power of his might. . . . For we wrestle not against flesh and blood, but against principalities, against powers, against the rulers of the darkness of this world, against spiritual wickedness in high places" (Eph. 6:10,12).

When he girded himself to run to the city of Jezreel, he took a humble place before King Ahab. He assumed a servant's place as one who wanted to honor his king. Though Elijah rebuked this monarch for his idolatry, he still honored him for the office he held.

Our Saviour's ministry was conducted in humility. We read in Philippians 2: "Let this mind be in you, which was also in Christ Jesus: who, being in the form of God, thought it not robbery to be equal with God: but made himself of no reputation" (vv. 5-7). Just prior to His death, our Lord showed this humble spirit when He washed the disciples' feet. This was a lesson to them and to all who call him Saviour and Lord—that they are to live and serve, not in pride but in humility.

Something of Ahab's character is seen in that he let Elijah run before the chariot. This man of God who had brought such a triumph that day should have been invited to sit with the king as he journeyed toward his home in Jezreel. In fact, Elijah should have been made prime minister, but Ahab cared nothing for the glory of God, even after the terrible judgment he had witnessed on Mount Carmel.

Elijah was undoubtedly hoping for a revival in Israel. This hope may have helped give him the extra strength to continue to run those many miles. He wanted to see what would happen when news of these events came to Jezebel, who was, in reality, the cause of idolatry in Israel. Perhaps she would turn to God as the people had when they cried out, "The Lord, he is the God; the Lord, he is the God" (I Kings 18:39).

On the surface, at least, Ahab seemed to have turned to God. He had consented to the death of Baal's prophets. He apparently did not raise a hand in protest as those wicked men were brought to judgment. He seemed to assent to all the things that took place on Mount Carmel; so Elijah must have felt there was the possibility of a real revival. No doubt the prophet hoped the day would end with Jezebel's realizing that she could not trifle with the things of God.

Elijah went no farther than the gate of the city, but Ahab went on to his palace and told Jezebel all that Elijah had done.

Possibly it was with a great degree of enthusiasm that he told his wife of the fire that fell from heaven and consumed the offering, the wood, the stones and even the dust and the water. After her own prophets had labored for six hours and nothing had happened, Elijah had prayed a brief prayer, and God had immediately answered. This was a miracle, indeed, and it caused the people to shout to the glory of God. Then he told her about the slaughter of the prophets of Baal. Perhaps there was a secret hope in his heart that she, too, would be convinced that she must honor God. He undoubtedly was convinced, but he was not saved. He knew what he ought to do, but he had no change of heart.

This is often the case with people. They become convinced of the truth of the Gospel, but they do not actually accept Christ as personal Saviour. Nicodemus was such a person, for he was convinced that the Lord Jesus could only do the things that He was doing because God was with Him. But our Lord told this Jewish leader that he needed to be born again. We cannot get away from that truth: "Except a man be born again, he cannot see the kingdom of God" (John 3:3).

There was a fatal omission in Ahab's narration of events. He told Jezebel all that Elijah had done but not what the Lord had done. The difference is simply this: Ahab was undoubtedly convinced that Elijah was a prophet of God, but since he himself was not born from above, he could not see that the events on Mount Carmel were the Lord's doing. Ahab praised a man. He probably told Jezebel how all the people were for Elijah. He showed how the authority of the priests of Baal had evaporated. Elijah had prayed that it would not rain, and it did not rain for three and a half years. He had also said that it would not rain until he asked God to make it rain, and this had taken place just as he said it would. In spite of this wealth of evidence, Jezebel was not convinced.

Jezebel's Threat

Perhaps Ahab was amazed at Jezebel's reactions. Her face probably became red with anger as she listened to how her prophets had died. Ahab was a weakling whom Jezebel easily stirred up to do what she wanted. In modern terms we would describe him as a henpecked husband who usually did what his wife told him to. Jezebel's vicious and vindictive character showed up in the message she sent to Elijah: "So let the gods do to me, and more also, if I make not thy life as the life of one of them by tomorrow about this time" (I Kings 19:2).

She was crafty and unscrupulous and merciless. Ahab was a weak tool in her hands. She was the foreshadowing of the religious woman spoken of in Revelation 2. There she is used as a symbol of an evil seducer, leading God's people astray: "Notwithstanding I have a few things against thee, because thou sufferest that woman Jezebel, which calleth herself a prophetess, to teach and to seduce my servants to commit fornication, and to eat things sacrificed unto idols. And I gave her space to repent of her fornication; and she repented not. Behold, I will cast her into a bed, and them that commit adultery with her into great tribulation, except they repent of their deeds" (vv. 20-22).

The Lord was addressing a church in apostolic days, but He was also speaking to much of the organized church of today, which is no longer teaching the truth of God but false doctrines.

Then in Revelation 17:3-5 we find the consummation of this system symbolized in the woman who sits on a scarlet -colored beast, the woman who is "Mystery, Babylon The Great, The Mother Of Harlots And Abominations Of The Earth."

Jezebel was insensitive to the presence of divine power, but her tongue was set on fire by hell. James said, "And the tongue is a fire, a world of iniquity: so is the tongue among our members, that it defileth the whole body, and setteth on fire the course of nature; and it is set on fire of hell" (James 3:6). She knew she could not harm the Lord, but she sought to take her revenge on God's chosen servant. Let us not forget that those who "live godly in Christ Jesus shall suffer persecution" (II Tim. 3:12).

Jezebel's Fear

Jezebel knew that God was almighty, and in spite of the fact that she threatened God's servant, she was afraid of him. She had the authority to send soldiers to take his life immediately, but her announcement gave him 24 hours to flee. Actually she did not dare lay a hand on him. Apparently she hoped that her threat would make him leave the country.

It is not unusual for people to put on a bold front with regard to spiritual things. It is only a front, however, for behind it is a heart of fear. Many are afraid to face the issues of life and eternity, and so they act as though they have resolved these matters and have no further concern with them.

Some years ago I conducted an evangelistic campaign in a church that did not want public invitations to be given. I announced, however, that anyone who wanted to talk to me about the Lord Jesus Christ and salvation should stay after the meeting. Among those who remained to speak to me was a young man whom I knew. I asked him, "Would you like to be saved?"

He answered, "No."

I then asked him why he had stayed to talk to me. He answered, "I am afraid to go to hell."

He did not want to be saved, but he was afraid of hell. I finally said to him, "I will be praying that God will make you willing to be saved."

At 12 o'clock that night he came to see me. By that time he wanted to be saved.

Let us not lie to ourselves and others concerning our spiritual fears. There is no point in trying to hide them from God, for He sees our hearts. We must turn to Him through faith in Christ and find the solution to our spiritual perplexities.

Elijah's reaction to Jezebel's threat was not consistent with his character. We would have expected him to demonstrate confidence in God. The promise in Isaiah is "Thou wilt keep him in perfect peace, whose mind is stayed on thee: because he trusteth in thee. Trust ye in the Lord for ever: for in the Lord Jehovah is everlasting strength" (26:3,4). But Elijah had no peace of mind or heart. He ran for his life.

Previous to this when he was confronted with danger, the word of God came to him very clearly. When Elijah's life was in danger for having told Ahab that it would not rain until he said so, God warned him to hide himself. When the brook dried up, he was instructed to go to Zarephath. Then, after three and a half years had passed, Elijah was instructed to show himself to Ahab because God was going to send rain. These orders were all clear and definite. But no word came to him from God concerning this threat. The prophet left on his own.

Had he not sought orders from God? Perhaps he did, but nothing in the record says he did. Elijah could not see behind the scenes; so he did not know what was going on in Jezebel's heart. He did not stop to think that if she had meant to kill him, she could have done so right then and there when she sent the messengers with the warning. Evidently there was a lesson Elijah needed to learn. He had stood up for God, but his success could have led to his destruction.

After Paul had been caught up into the third heaven and received wonderful revelations from God, he received a thorn in the flesh. God allowed this to come lest elation and pride, because of the great revelations given him, would lead him astray (II Cor. 12:7-10).

Elijah had successfully consummated one of the greatest feats in history. It is true that God did it through him, but Elijah was the instrument, and there was the grave danger that he might become proud. This is a danger that always confronts people who are successful servants of the Lord.

Satan has caught many of them off guard and has succeeded in causing their withdrawal from effective service. The principle involved is illustrated well in the case of Saul, Israel's first king. Samuel, speaking for the Lord, said, "When thou wast little in thine own sight, wast thou not made the head of the tribes of Israel, and the Lord anointed thee king over Israel? And the Lord sent thee on a journey, and said, Go and utterly destroy the sinners the Amalekites, and fight against them until they be consumed" (I Sam. 15:17,18).

Saul fought the Amalekites, but he did not obey God with reference to their complete destruction. So he was rejected for his pride and rebellion.

Three Possible Reasons

There were possibly three major reasons why the Lord temporarily allowed Elijah to follow his own devices. God did not desert him but temporarily withdrew Himself, first for Elijah's own sake. He did not want His servant to become a victim of pride and be useless to Him. Elijah needed to see that by himself he could not do the work of God. Pride is subtle, and unless it is checked it can end our usefulness.

The second reason was possibly that God intended to discipline Israel because they had not returned to Him with their whole heart. They had to reap the fruit of their own sowing. If Elijah had stayed with them, his presence might have stood in the way of their just punishment.

In the third place, God possibly wanted to take Elijah to a solitary place where He could speak to him alone and reveal Himself to him in a fresh way. He could have done this by a specific command, but apparently Elijah reached a decision before God's will was made clear to him, and this is why he ran.

Elijah was not forsaken. His experience reminds us that whom the Lord loves He chastens and that if we are not chastened, we are not sons (Heb. 12:5-10). Regardless of how chastening comes, it is not at the moment a joyous experience but a grievous one (v. 11). "Afterward it yieldeth the peaceable fruit of righteousness unto them which are exercised thereby" (v. 11).

Elijah first came to Beer-sheba, which was in Judah, and left his servant there. This was outside of Ahab's kingdom. The prophet continued a day's journey into the wilderness, sat down under a juniper tree and asked God to let him die.

God dealt gently with His servant and sent an angel to awaken him and have him eat. Elijah was refreshed and strengthened and lay down and slept once more. The second time the angel came to him and said, "Arise and eat; because the journey is too great for thee" (I Kings 19:7).

Elijah must have realized then that he had depended on his own intellect and discernment. He was a man of such faith that he had seen and heard the rain before it ever fell. Yet he was only human, after all, a man of like passions as we are. Through the psalmist the Lord promised, "I will instruct thee and teach thee in the way which thou shalt go: I will guide thee with mine eye" (Ps. 32:8). We need to depend on God's wisdom, not our own.

Trusting in what he thought looked good led to Lot's downfall. "And Lot lifted up his eyes, and beheld all the plain of Jordan, that it was well watered every where, before the Lord destroyed Sodom and Gomorrah, even as the garden of the Lord, like the land of Egypt, as thou comest unto Zoar. Then Lot chose him all the plain of Jordan; and Lot journeyed east: and they separated themselves the one from the other" (Gen. 13:10,11). According to the record, Lot took several downward steps, and each one of them was the result of relying on his own wisdom.

The case of the 12 spies who were sent to the land is another illustration of how people look at things from their own viewpoint and do not see these things as God sees them. The account is given in Numbers 13. Ten of the spies came back with this report: "And there we saw the giants, the sons of Anak, which come of the giants: and we were in our own sight as grasshoppers, and so we were in their sight" (v. 33). Their decision was reached on the basis of what they saw — not on what God wanted them to see.

When a person views things as God does, he chooses a way of life in line with God's desires. We read that Moses forsook Egypt by faith, "not fearing the wrath of the king: for he endured, as seeing him who is invisible" (Heb. 11:27). Faith gave Moses vision that went beyond what the human eye can see. This was the happy experience of Job at the end of his trials, for he said, "I have heard of thee by the hearing of the ear: but now mine eye seeth thee" (Job 42:5).

Job had a new vision of the Lord; he understood why things were as they were, and he abhored himself and repented in dust and ashes (v. 6).

Elijah, when he received the threat from Jezebel, looked at it with human reason and ran for his life. This time he did not run for the Lord. His steps were uncertain this time. He apparently had no divine direction, no word from God as to where he should go. Let us always be careful to follow the path that God has laid out for us.

Some people tell us that a need constitutes a call. But if that were the case, some of us would have to be 100 persons, instead of one. Here at Back to the Bible we receive hundreds of letters telling us of a great need. These needs are all around us, but we must know from God what particular need we are to meet. In this way our steps are sure, and we will certainly be doing the work God wants us to do. Otherwise, we would be working in circles, and the work of God would not be done.

The following song by Mary Slade pictures for us the blessings that become ours when we closely follow the Lord.

Footsteps of Jesus

Sweetly, Lord, have we heard Thee calling,
　"Come, follow Me!"
And we see where Thy footprints falling
　Lead us to Thee.

Tho they lead o'er the cold, dark mountains,
　Seeking His sheep,
Or along by Siloam's fountains,
　Helping the weak:

If they lead thru the temple holy,
  Preaching the Word,
Or in homes of the poor and lowly,
  Serving the Lord:

Then at last, when on high He sees us,
  Our journey done,
We will rest where the steps of Jesus
End at His throne.

Footprints of Jesus,
  That make the pathway glow!
We will follow the steps of Jesus
  Where'er they go.

Not Forsaken

Servants of God who have great zeal and courage for God and His truth become weak and timid when left to themselves. This may explain why so many Christians are weak and timid today. Do we not know that all things are possible with God and that without Him nothing is possible?

We can praise God that He does not forsake His people. He is faithful to us and watches over us though He gives no visible manifestations of His presence. The Israelites did not enter the Promised Land when they should have; yet God did not forsake them though He temporarily removed His hand of blessing. He assured them, "Be strong and of a good courage, fear not, nor be afraid of them: for the Lord thy God, he it is that doth go with thee; he will not fail thee, nor forsake thee" (Deut. 31:6).

When Moses was about to die, he called Joshua and said in the presence of all Israel: "Be strong and of a good courage: for thou must go with this people unto the land which the Lord hath sworn unto their fathers to give them; and thou shalt cause them to inherit it" (v. 7). God's promise to us is "I will never leave thee, nor forsake thee" (Heb. 13:5). The patriarch Job suffered the loss of his family, his wealth and his health; yet he was never forsaken by God.

Our Lord is the only one serving God who was ever forsaken. He cried out while on the cross, "My God, my God, why hast thou forsaken me?" (Ps. 22:1). He was forsaken so that we who turn to God through faith in Him would never be forsaken.

Even though we may forget it, God never forgets that "we have this treasure [the Gospel] in earthen vessels, that the excellency of the power may be of God, and not of us" (II Cor. 4:7). This is why He told us that He has chosen that which the world calls foolish, weak and base (see I Cor. 1:26-29). Through such He glorifies His own name. This is why Paul reminded us that none of us in our work for the Lord is anything; only God counts, for He gives the increase. "So then neither is he that planteth any thing, neither he that watereth; but God that giveth the increase" (3:7).

Someone has said, "The best of men are but men at their best." God wants us to know this: Let God's power be withdrawn, even for a moment, and one sees that people are only earthen vessels — absolutely valueless and useless in themselves. This is why the psalmist said, " Verily every man at his best state is altogether vanity" (Ps. 39:5). Man left to himself is a failure. Ecclesiastes 7:20 says, "For there is not a just man upon earth, that doeth good, and sinneth not."

Noah, left to himself, got drunk. Lot, left to himself, became carnal. Abraham, when he did not depend on God, lied concerning his wife. Moses forgot for a moment where his strength lay and became angry. Aaron failed to remember that God had assigned different responsibilities to his servants; so he became jealous. Joshua became careless and hasty in his decision with regard to Ai and also the Gibeonites. David committed adultery and murder. Peter became self-sufficient and denied his Lord. These things happen to us as soon as we, even for a short while, leave God out of our lives.

In order to give us lasting examples and instruction, God had recorded for us the experiences of these people. Paul told us this in I Corinthians 10:11-13: "Now all these things happened unto them [the Israelites] for ensamples: and they are written for our admonition, upon whom the ends of the world are come. Wherefore let him that thinketh he standeth take heed lest he fall. There hath no temptation taken you but such as is common to man: but God is faithful, who will not suffer you to be tempted above that ye are able; but will with the temptation also make a way to escape, that ye may be able to bear it." Just because others fail we don't need to fail. God has given us these examples so that we might be forewarned and forearmed, entrusting ourselves to His keeping and distrusting our own strength.

Still, we find it very easy to criticize another servant of God. When he falls or falters, we tend to find fault with him. What we often forget is that the testings others face may be far greater than what we ourselves have to cope with. It is our responsibility to pray for fellow believers and uphold them before the Lord.

We must, then, be sympathetic with Elijah, for he was but a man. He wanted to give up just as we sometimes are tempted to give up. God, however, never gives up. The Lord wants His own character to be seen in us, and He will make this possible if we will just lean on Him. Paul wrote to the Corinthians: "Therefore, my beloved brethren, be ye stedfast, unmoveable, always abounding in the work of the Lord, forasmuch as ye know that your labour is not in vain in the Lord" (15:58).

I have met servants of God who have allowed circumstances alone to direct their path. At such times I have felt that what they were doing was not in the will of God for them, but what could I say? Sometimes they approached me apologetically and sought to justify what they were doing, declaring that they were having good opportunities to witness for the Lord. Yet they knew and I knew that such was not the case. My heart was heavy for them.

The exercise of faith must be constant as we walk with God. We do not exercise faith in this aspect of salvation once for all. For the new birth, we trust Christ once for all and are born into His family. Then "there is therefore now no condemnation to them which are in Christ Jesus" (Rom. 8:1). Only after we are born again can we walk with God, but this must be done in the power of the Spirit.

Our Christian walk is a daily walk, a step at a time. It is a life of faith lived moment by moment. Faith itself is a divine gift from God and comes through the Word of God. "Faith cometh by hearing, and hearing by the word of God" (Rom. 10:17). So Galatians 2:20 is appropriate again: "I am crucified with Christ: nevertheless I live; yet not I, but Christ liveth in me: and the life which I now live in the flesh I live by the faith of the Son of God, who loved me, and gave himself for me."

Elijah's Depression

Elijah traveled on foot about 95 miles to the southern border of Judah. Then he went another day's journey into the wilderness. By that time he was completely exhausted. He had remarkable physical strength and endurance, but he had extended himself to the breaking point. He had first prepared for the "showdown" with the prophets of Baal at Mount Carmel. There was great pressure on him because of satanic opposition while he was on the mountain. Then it was necessary to kill the prophets of Baal. Such invasion of Satan's territory is not done easily. Then Elijah prayed for rain with great earnestness, and finally he ran about 16 miles to Jezreel to see what results would follow the great triumph at Mount Carmel. All of this took place in one day.

Satan knows that a tired body is an added opportunity for him, and he took advantage of it in this case. When Jezebel threatened Elijah, he seemed to lose control and continued running until he sat under the juniper tree in the wilderness.

Then he requested that he might die. He felt his labors had been fruitless. He longed for rest. "It is enough," he said (I Kings 19:4). He had hoped to see a great revival, but no spiritual change had taken place in Israel.

I must admit that there are times when I have wondered after many years of radio broadcasting to millions of people just what has been accomplished. God has called us to faithfulness, however, not to success. My hope and trust lie in Him. Is this how you trust Him for the work He has given you to do?

Some men in the Bible went even further than Elijah did in discouragement. Jeremiah said, "Cursed be the day wherein I was born" (Jer. 20:14). Job wished that the day of his birth might perish (see Job 3:3). These men all had natures like ours. They showed what they could be when God filled them and controlled them and also what they were when left to themselves. If we did not have this knowledge, we would be tempted to think they were superhuman instead of ordinary people like the rest of us.

How inconsistent we can be when we are not walking with the Lord! When Elijah fled from Jezebel, he fled "for his life" (I Kings 19:3). Under the juniper tree he pleaded, "Lord, take away my life" (v. 4). Life, however, is precious to each of us, and Elijah was no exception. The picture was not all bad with regard to this man of God, for in his dejection he turned to the Lord. Though he was still depressed, he unburdened his heart before God.

How often when things have gone wrong have we turned away from the Lord in dejection and depression! Sometimes we have even accused Him of mistreating us. But Elijah didn't do this. He was on speaking terms with the Lord, though God did not answer his request for death. He had asked amiss; he was not praying in the Spirit. In fact, Elijah never died, for God took him to heaven without dying.

God knew that His servant had overtaxed himself and needed a renewal of his physical life as well as his spiritual life. Our inner life is very sensitive to our outward condition. Rest is very important to all of us. Proper exercise is also important. We sometimes forget this, but God does not. Our physical condition can influence our spiritual condition.

Elijah felt very much alone. He admitted this to God: "I, even I only, am left" (v. 10). Loneliness sometimes is a penalty that people pay for being great. Someone sent me the following paragraph:

"A leader is a lonely man. He follows visions that others cannot see. He moves ahead when others lag behind. He walks in solitude with God. Driven on by burning desire to achieve goals that to others seem visionary or impractical (because leaders are not conformists), they are looked upon with suspicion by the run-of-the-mill crowd. Men who lead are certain targets for the biting barbs of criticism. Their fearless, clear, compelling manner makes them a prey to those who do not understand them. But the church needs leaders today—men who will bear criticism, who will bear reproach for the cause of Christ; men who will stand up when others fall, who will go on when others faint. Will you be a leader?"

God does not leave such men without help however. The following poem is a testimony to the faithfulness of the women who have stood behind many Christian workers and helped them in difficult places.

There is one person in your church
  Who knows your preacher's life.
She's wept and smiled and prayed with him.
  And that's your preacher's wife!

She knows one prophet's weakest point,
  And knows his greatest power;
She's heard him speak in trumpet tone,
  In his great triumph hour.

She's heard him groaning in his soul,
  When bitter raged the strife,
As hand in his she knelt with him
  For she's a preacher's wife.

You tell your tales of prophets brave,
  Who walked across the world
And changed the course of history
  By burning words they hurled.

And I will tell how back of them
  Some women lived their lives,
Who wept with them and smiled with them.
  They were the preachers' wives!

Shortly after the Back to the Bible Broadcast began, a day came when I was very discouraged. I walked the floor saying, "What is the use? We cannot go on this way." My wife suddenly realized that the Devil was trying to get both of us discouraged, and she said she would not give in. She went to be alone with God and to search the Scriptures for a message from Him. He gave her this verse from Job: "Though he slay me, yet will I trust in him" (13:15). God used this verse to lead us out of that period of despondency. Let us not be too hard on Elijah for becoming discouraged.

When Elijah had his eyes on the Lord, he faced his foes without fear. But the moment he forgot God and concentrated on the circumstances, things changed. He looked at the danger and lost his courage. Centuries later Peter did the same thing. As long as he looked at the Lord, he walked on the water and was not afraid. The moment he looked at the waves, he became afraid and began to sink.

Someone reading this may be living under difficult circumstances. Perhaps you are living with an ungodly husband whose temper flares up constantly. Perhaps you feel you cannot take it any longer. Look to Jesus instead of the circumstances that are affecting you so badly, and the Lord will give you strength. Trust Him to save your husband.

Or maybe you are living in some situation that you could not avoid, and yet you feel it is impossible to continue in it. Look to Jesus, and then you can see your circumstances from the right perspective.

God looked on His servant Elijah with kindness and provided food for him. The Lord did not forget him. He followed him everywhere. Elijah learned as we should learn: "He [God] hath not dealt with us after our sins; nor rewarded us according to our iniquities. For as the heaven is high above the earth, so great is his mercy toward them that fear him. As far as the east is from the west, so far hath he removed our transgressions from us. Like as a father pitieth his children, so the Lord pitieth them that fear him. For he knoweth our frame; he remembereth that we are dust" (Ps. 103:10-14).

The message of the following poem may speak to your heart as it has to mine:

Hast thou been hungry, child of mine?
    I, too, have needed bread.
For forty days I tasted naught
    Till by the angels fed.
Hast thou been thirsty?
    On the cross I suffered thirst for thee;
I have promised to supply thy need
    My child, come unto me.

Perhaps thy way is weary oft,
    Thy feet grow tired and lame.
I wearied when I reached the well,
    I suffered just the same.
And when I bore the heavy cross
    I fainted 'neath the load.
And so I have promised rest to all
    Who walk the weary road.

Does Satan sometimes buffet thee
    And tempt thy soul to sin?
Do faith and hope and love grow weak
    Are doubts and fears within?
Remember I was tempted thrice
    By this same foe of thine,
But he could not resist the Word
    Nor conquer power divine.

When thou art sad and tears fall fast,
    My heart goes out to thee
For I wept o'er Jerusalem,
    The place so dear to me.
And when I came to Lazarus' tomb I wept,
    My heart was sore.
I will comfort thee when thou dost weep
    'Til sorrow all is o'er.

Do hearts prove false when thine is true?
   I know that bitter dart;
I was betrayed by one I loved,
   I died of a broken heart.
I loved my own, they loved me not;
   My heart was lonely, too.
I'll never leave thee child of mine
   My loving heart is true.

Art thou discouraged in thy work?
   Does misery seem vain?
I ministered midst unbelief
   With those of greed of gain.
They would not hearken to My voice
   But scoffed with one accord,
Your labor never is in vain
   If done unto the Lord.

So have courage, then, My faithful one;
   I suffered all the way.
Thy sensitive and loving heart
   I understand today.
Whate'er thy grief, whate'er thy care
   Just bring it unto Me.
Yea, in thy day of trouble, call;
   I will deliver thee!

Elijah had lost hope of seeing the people of Israel return to the Lord. Thus life no longer was attractive to him. When hope is gone, life is not worth living. Perhaps it seemed to Elijah that the Lord had given up also, but this was not the case. The Lord did not answer the prayer of His discouraged servant when he asked to die.

The present world has no answer to the turmoil and strife going on in its midst, but the Church is not without hope. Our hope lies in the coming of our Lord. This we must never forget.

Chapter 9

God's Kindness to His Servant

We learn from the New Testament, "There hath no temptation taken you but such as is common to man: but God is faithful, who will not suffer [permit] you to be tempted above that ye are able; but will with the temptation also make a way to escape, that ye may be able to bear it" (I Cor. 10:13). Perhaps we think our testings are different from those experienced by others, but this is not true. They are common to all people. Circumstances may differ for us, but the tests are the same. Not all of us may run from someone like Jezebel, but we are subject to fear and discouragement regardless of the cause.

How comforting to realize that God knows us intimately. The psalmist declared long ago, "Like as a father pitieth his children, so the Lord pitieth them that fear him. For he knoweth our frame; he remembereth that we are dust" (Ps. 103:13,14). The Lord will either lighten the burden, or He will increase our strength so that we can bear it.

Another promise of great encouragement to me personally is II Timothy 2:12,13: "If we suffer, we shall also reign with him: if we deny him, he also will deny us: if we believe not, yet he abideth faithful: he cannot deny himself." Elijah failed temporarily to exercise faith, but God did not abandon His servant. God is faithful to His own.

He did not remove the wicked Queen Jezebel immediately. Neither did He do some mighty work in Israel. He did, however, make a way of escape for His dejected servant, giving him the strength he needed.

114

God's eye had followed every step that Elijah had taken. He did not love the prophet less than when he stood in victory on Mount Carmel. God's love is not based on our ability. He will not fail us at any time. His promise is "I will never leave thee, nor forsake thee. So that we may boldly say, The Lord is my helper, and I will not fear what man shall do unto me" (Heb. 13:5,6).

God does not condone or encourage sin in a believer's life. He did not approve of Elijah's wish for death as a means of rest. But God empathized with His child and gave him the physical help he needed. God gave His beloved sleep just as the psalmist said He would (see Ps. 127:2). Elijah found that though weeping may endure for a night, joy comes in the morning (see 30:5).

Good, wholesome, restful sleep is a blessing from God. What healing and strength lie in becoming unconscious for a time to the things around us. God watched over His servant, and his mind and heart were quieted and given peace.

What do we do in wakeful night hours? Someone asked me that one time. One of the first things I love to do is pray. Sometimes I recite some of the Scripture verses I have memorized. There are occasions when that is not sufficient; so I go to my study and spend an hour or more studying my Bible. There have been times when I have spent four or five hours in this manner, depending on what God was seeking to do in my heart.

These have always been precious times. I found that God awakened me to speak to me and deal with my soul in a way that He could not at other times.

This is what He did for Elijah. "And as he lay and slept under a juniper tree, behold, then an angel touched him, and said unto him, Arise and eat. And he looked, and, behold, there was a cake baken on the coals, and a cruse of water at his head. And he did eat and drink, and laid him down again. And the angel of the Lord came again the second time, and touched him, and said, Arise and eat; because the journey is too great for thee" (I Kings 19:5-7).

115

Ministry of Angels

Elijah still had a great distance to go, but God watched over him as he slept. He was not forsaken but was provided for through rest and food for a journey that would cover many more miles. Here we have a demonstration of the ministry of angels to those who are the elect of the Lord. God's tender care is expressed through the ministry of angels, who are servants of those who are heirs of salvation. The same angels who delight to witness God's majesty and greatness also enjoy ministering to God's saints on the earth.

This action on the part of God is typical of His nature as the God of grace. He takes no account of our worthiness or unworthiness. His grace is free and sovereign. He loves His own, and He loves them to the end.

Can you imagine an angel doing such a lowly task as cooking a meal for a discouraged saint of God, when that angel's regular assignment was to stand in the presence of almighty God and see Him in His majesty and glory? There was no grumbling on the part of this messenger — he loved to do what he did.

When Lot was living in Sodom, an angel came to warn him and to get him out of that wicked and doomed city. Daniel was cast into the lions' den, but an angel was with him, sent by God to shut the mouths of the ferocious beasts.

When Lazarus the beggar died, angels carried him into Abraham's bosom. When Peter was thrown into prison and the authorities planned to put him to death, an angel came by night, awakened him and helped him escape from prison. An angel stood by Paul when the ship he was on was about to go to pieces and assured the apostle that God would save the life of every person on board.

The ministry of angels is wonderful to consider. I believe God has assigned an angel to each of His own. We are engaged in a spiritual warfare against evil forces and are adequately prepared with the help sufficient for victory.

Angels play an important role with regard to children. We read in Matthew 18:10: "Take heed that ye despise not one of

116

these little ones; for I say unto you, That in heaven their angels do always behold the face of my Father which is in heaven." I believe God has assigned a special angel to each child.

The psalmist wrote: "For he shall give his angels charge over thee, to keep thee in all thy ways" (Ps. 91:11). This was written concerning the person who "dwelleth in the secret place of the most High," the person who fears God (v. 1).

Another precious promise is found in Psalm 34:7: "The angel of the Lord encampeth round about them that fear him, and delivereth them." This is provision made by God. Angels are sent to minister with God's purposes in view. It is no wonder, then, that God sent an angel to minister to His servant Elijah and to prepare him for a long journey he had to take. The prophet went to Mount Horeb, the same mountain on which Moses had met God. Perhaps Elijah thought of Moses and his experience when he presented himself to the Children of Israel and they rejected him. Then Moses had to flee from Egypt and go deep into the desert, but that was where God met him. This is what Elijah apparently was looking for also.

At times each of us feels that a different environment would make things easier for us. We will see, in Elijah's case, what a change in environment did for him, though he could have had the same experience if he had stayed in Israel. God did not forsake him. Elijah needed spiritual refreshing. He needed to get away from the duties of life for a while and be alone with the Lord. Our Saviour did this quite often when he prayed.

God allowed his servant to take this long, hard journey across the desert and in grace provided for him and accompanied him. Whether or not Elijah was actually doing God's will at this time, his motive was certainly that of seeking to put God first. The Lord did not forsake him, and He will not forsake us.

We read in I Kings 19:8 that Elijah "arose, and did eat and drink, and went in the strength of that meat forty days and forty nights unto Horeb the mount of God." Again Elijah experienced the superhuman strength provided by the Lord.

He Giveth More Grace

He giveth more grace when the burdens grow greater;
He sendeth more strength when the labors increase.
To added affliction He addeth His mercy;
To multiplied trials, His multiplied peace.

When we have exhausted our store of endurance,
When our strength has failed ere the day is half done,
When we reach the end of our hoarded resources,
Our Father's full giving is only begun.

His love has no limit, His grace has no measure,
His pow'r has no boundary known unto men;
For out of His infinite riches in Jesus,
He giveth, and giveth, and giveth again!
— Annie Johnson Flint

Like Elijah we all have times of discouragement. None of us are immune. Pastors are often targets of the Enemy in this respect. They preach faithfully for the Lord but see little response, if any, in the hearts of the hearers. Less important things begin to take the time of the members of their congregation. Sunday night attendance dwindles. People have little interest in prayer meetings. And the average Christian seems to have lost his zeal for witnessing to those who are unsaved.

Regardless of the cause of our discouragement, let us learn from Elijah's experience that God is never discouraged. He never gives up. When God has given us the responsibility for some work or obligation, let us learn not to give up either.

Sometimes God's plans do not coincide with our plans. Not all of His plans are short range; many of them are long range. Though he did not realize it at the time, Elijah was fitting into part of God's long-range plan for Israel.

God's Love for Elijah

When Elijah was discouraged, he received God's love in a very special way. God did not rebuke His tired and depressed servant but provided food, rest, protection, comfort and strength through an angel.

If he had not learned it before, Elijah learned that God's love is constant. Perhaps he may have feared that he had forfeited that love by running away from Jezebel and her threats, but God still loved him. The love of God never changes, even though our awareness of it does. The sun still shines even though it may disappear from view behind clouds or appear to go down at night.

The love of God is like that. We may not always be aware of God's love, but it surrounds us. Circumstances may surround us like a cloud or like night, but God's love is not changed. It is still with us.

Elijah also learned that God's love is sometimes manifested in a very special way to meet special needs in our lives. There is no mention of an angel when Elijah was cared for at the brook Cherith. No angel is mentioned concerning his stay with the widow at Zarephath. Something more was needed after this fall by Elijah. God's holiness is offended by sin, but He remembers our nature. In Elijah's case, in order to assure the prophet that he was still loved and to bring him to the place of repentance and usefulness, God sent an angel to help him.

We can see this in Peter's experience. After he had denied the Lord three times, he wept in bitterness at his own weakness and carnality. The Lord did not leave him in that condition. The women who went to the tomb on the morning of the resurrection were told by a young man clothed in a long, white garment: "Be not affrighted: Ye seek Jesus of Nazareth, which was crucified: he is risen; he is not here: behold the place where they laid him. But go your way, tell his disciples and Peter that he goeth before you into Galilee: there shall ye see him, as he said unto you" (Mark 16:6,7). The very fact that Peter was singled out here was a message of love to him. God's love is a giving type of love. Our affection and consideration for people may be shaken by circumstances because basically we are selfish. God's love is just the opposite; He is constantly giving and does not change.

119

"While we were yet sinners, Christ died for us" (Rom. 5:8). The Lord went out after the wandering sheep and carried it home (see Luke 15:3-7). When the Prodigal Son returned, a feast was prepared for him (see vv. 11-24). All this illustrates the special love of God for the sinner. God hates our sin, but He yearns over us with tender, unchanging love. God, who gave His only begotten Son for us, will allow nothing to separate us from His love.

The Williams translation of Romans 8:31-39 says, "What are we then to say to facts like these? If God is for us, who can be against us? Since He did not spare His own Son but gave Him up for us all, will He not with Him graciously give us everything else? Who can bring any charge against those whom God has chosen? It is God who declared them in right standing; who can condemn them? Christ Jesus who died, or rather, who was raised from the dead, is now at God's right hand, and is actually pleading for us. Who can separate us from Christ's love? Can suffering or misfortune or persecution or hunger or destitution or danger or the sword? As the Scripture says: 'For your sake we are being put to death the livelong day; we are treated like sheep to be slaughtered.' And yet in all these things we keep on gloriously conquering through Him who loved us. For I have full assurance that neither death nor life nor angels nor principalities nor the present nor the future nor evil forces above or beneath, nor anything else in all creation, will be able to separate us from the love of God as shown in Christ Jesus our Lord."

The Apostle Paul closed Romans 11 with these words: "How fathomless the depths of God's resources, wisdom, and knowledge! How unsearchable His decisions, and how mysterious His methods! For who has ever understood the thoughts of the Lord, or has ever been His adviser? Or who has ever advanced God anything to have Him pay him back? For from Him everything comes, through Him everything lives, and for Him everything exists. Glory to Him forever! Amen" (vv. 33-36, Williams).

The third fact Elijah learned concerning the love of God is that His love endures. Using an angel as His messenger, God first provided Elijah with food. He had been traveling for a long time in the desert. After he slept for a while, the angel awakened him and gave him a meal. Then after a good, long rest, possibly early in the morning, the angel came again and awakened Elijah and told him to arise and eat because the journey was too long for him. God's love never stops. It is long-suffering and kind. It endures all things and will never fail. After he had rested and was refreshed, Elijah was ready for the next phase of his ministry.

God offers us, after our day's task is finished, food that is more than physical. In the morning, before our day's work begins, He provides fresh bread from His Word for our nourishment and strength.

This is spoken of many times in the Scriptures. Isaiah commented on this, "Hast thou not known? hast thou not heard, that the everlasting God, the Lord, the Creator of the ends of the earth, fainteth not, neither is weary? there is no searching of his understanding. He giveth power to the faint; and to them that have no might he increaseth strength. Even the youths shall faint and be weary, and the young men shall utterly fall: but they that wait upon the Lord shall renew their strength; they shall mount up with wings as eagles; they shall run, and not be weary; and they shall walk, and not faint" (Isa. 40:28-31).

Elijah arose and ate and went in the strength of the food provided for 40 days and 40 nights. When he reached Horeb, the mount of God, "he came thither unto a cave, and lodged there; and, behold, the word of the Lord came to him, and he said unto him, What doest thou here, Elijah?" (I Kings 19:9). This question was designed to stir up Elijah's thinking about his present situation and future ministry.

This was a long distance from the scenes of his labors in Israel. He had traveled about 95 miles to the juniper tree, and from there he had traveled about 200 miles more through the desert to reach the place where Moses had stayed while a fugitive from the Egyptians. Perhaps Elijah felt that in this place he would be able to speak with God as Moses had done many years before.

Elijah was not in the will of God when he fled from Jezebel, but apparently the Lord directed his steps to Horeb in order to make him useful again. Nevertheless, he had all of those miles to retrace. God is sovereign in His grace and did not forsake His servant in his hour of need.

Chapter 10

Elijah at Horeb

The distance Elijah traveled to Horeb, under normal conditions, could have been covered in seven or eight days. Why it took him longer we are not told, but it reminds us of the Israelites' wandering in the desert for 40 years to complete a journey that could have been made in a few weeks.

As Elijah approached the lofty heights of this great mountain, he must have been reminded of the remarkable dealings of God with Moses and the Israelites at this place. Here God met Moses at the burning bush. Then later when the Israelites were liberated and on their way to Canaan, God gave them the Law here. This was the same mountain where Moses interceded for his people that they might not be destroyed. Here they were victorious over Amalek, and here they experienced the miracle of water coming from the rock. Although Elijah received no commandment to go to Horeb, he must have been directed there by the providence of God.

We need to remind ourselves of what the Bible teaches concerning God's care for His children. In one place we read: "A man's heart deviseth his way: but the Lord directeth his steps" (Prov. 16:9). In another place God says, "Man's goings are of the Lord; how can a man then understand his own way?" (20:24). The hearts of people are under God's control, for Proverbs 21:1,2 says, "The king's heart is in the hand of the Lord, as the rivers of water: he turneth it whithersoever he will. Every way of a man is right in his own eyes: but the

123

Lord pondereth the hearts." God knew the heart of Elijah, and He knew that Elijah was still vitally concerned about heavenly things and the honor of his God.

While he was alone in the cave, possibly thinking that he was forsaken, God asked him, "What doest thou here, Elijah?" (I Kings 19:9). God was right there with him in spite of all the fear and strain that Elijah had labored under.

The passage says that the "word of the Lord" came to Elijah. This reminds us of John 1:1, which reads: "In the beginning was the Word, and the Word was with God, and the Word was God." This could have been none other than the second Person of the Trinity, the Lord Jesus Christ Himself, who spoke with Elijah.

The question "What doest thou here, Elijah?" was an appeal to the conscience. This type of question leads to self-examination. We should open our hearts to the Lord and let Him ask this same question of us. None can escape the ever-present examination of the Lord. He has a right to ask, "What are you doing here?"

We learn from Proverbs 15:3: "The eyes of the Lord are in every place, beholding the evil and the good." A further truth is added concerning this in II Chronicles 16:9: "For the eyes of the Lord run to and fro throughout the whole earth, to shew himself strong in the behalf of them whose heart is perfect toward him."

Elijah's answer to God's inquiry was very frank. He did not seek to evade the question. He said, "I have been very jealous for the Lord God of hosts: for the children of Israel have forsaken thy covenant, thrown down thine altars, and slain thy prophets with the sword; and I, even I only, am left; and they seek my life, to take it away" (I Kings 19:10).

Elijah admitted his thoughts of his own hopelessness. Everything he said was true, but he did not know the truth about everything in connection with his own life. He was not aware of God's far-reaching plan for himself and Israel. He had to learn that God does not necessarily fulfill His whole plan in the lifetime of one man. One servant may add one part to God's work, and another may add another part. All of these parts put together make up the whole. This was what God was getting ready to teach Elijah.

Yet, how many of us could answer God's question "What are you doing here?" with honesty. How zealous are we about spiritual things? Are we cold, hot or lukewarm?

God's reply to Elijah's answer was "Go forth, and stand upon the mount before the Lord. And, behold, the Lord passed by, and a great and strong wind rent the mountains, and brake in pieces the rocks before the Lord; but the Lord was not in the wind: and after the wind an earthquake; but the Lord was not in the earthquake: and after the earthquake a fire; but the Lord was not in the fire: and after the fire a still small voice" (vv. 11,12).

What would our answer be to the command "Go forth. Stand before the Lord." Too many of us take a negative approach to these deep and serious things in life. We talk about the sins, depravity and wickedness of the world, but what are we doing to reach people for Christ?

Today we speak about our nation's moral decline. We criticize the world and look with displeasure at our young people. What do we do about it all? Like Elijah, we need a new vision of the Lord. We need to come out of the cave of darkness and stand before God.

The next few words in this chapter tell us, "The Lord passed by" (v. 11). Elijah remained in the cave during the time of this great storm and earthquake and fire, all of which demonstrated the power of God. This was very much like the time when God spoke to Moses on the mount and the people of Israel were terrified at the demonstration of God's power in the elements.

God's Grace

God, however, did not speak in the wind or in the earthquake or in the fire. He did not speak to Elijah from the standpoint of the Law but rather from the standpoint of grace. The still, small voice speaks not of legal requirements but of God's grace.

When Elijah heard God speak, he "wrapped his face in his mantle, and went out, and stood in the entering in of the cave. And, behold, there came a voice unto him, and said, What doest thou here, Elijah?" (v. 13). Not the Law but grace broke his heart. It is the goodness of God that leads us to repentance (see Rom. 2:4). Once more Elijah repeated what we have already quoted from verse 10, but now the Lord is ready to recommission him.

Elijah finally realized all was not lost. Though God spoke through the great demonstrations of nature, He was still going to speak to His people in grace. The thunder and the fire and the earthquake brought fear, but only grace brings true revival.

Too often we seek great demonstrations, crowds and all kinds of activity, but God brings about revival through dealing with the individual in the quietness of grace. The thunders of judgment are necessary, but the still, small voice of the Gospel is what penetrates the hearts of people.

In a very real sense Elijah had been a voice of thunder and fire to Israel. Like John the Baptist, who later thundered the message of repentance, Elijah had warned a nation in rebellion against God. He was recommissioned to still speak in that manner, and yet, at the same time, a promise of grace was given for those who would respond.

Elijah Provided For

God spoke to Elijah as He did in order to prepare him for a new commission. Though it was many years later that Peter penned his epistle, what he wrote will help us as we think about Elijah. The truth given by Peter most certainly was in God's mind concerning His servant of old. "According as his divine power hath given unto us all things that pertain unto life and godliness, through the knowledge of him that hath called us to glory and virtue [energy, efficiency]" (II Pet. 1:3). God never leaves us without properly equipping us for the work we are to do.

We can apply these truths to Elijah and find God saying, in effect, "Elijah, you need not be despondent or run from Me.

There is no need for you to be afraid. I am your God and have given you all that is essential and necessary for life. Jezebel will not be able to take your life. I have made ample provision for your spiritual growth and development. Remember the blessings of past days — the brook and the ravens, the barrel and the cruse of oil, the fire that fell from heaven when you asked for it and the rain that fell through your prayers. Remember, Elijah, I am the God who made all of this possible. I am your God and have provided everything you need."

Perhaps we have felt like Elijah and said, "What is the use?" Perhaps we have given the best of our lives to accomplish something for the Lord and feel that we have been left stranded. Perhaps we feel that the Enemy is seeking to destroy all traces of Christianity and belief in the true God and that he is after our soul too. Perhaps we feel we are the only one left of all God's people. If so, we need to be reminded, as Elijah was, that God still had 7000 who had not bowed their knee to Baal. And God still is the Almighty God. He is still on His throne. People cannot dethrone Him, no matter how hard they try. All we need for life and godliness and Christian service is found in Him.

Perhaps we have tried hard to overcome temptations and to rise above our testings. Perhaps we have fought against the overwhelming odds of modernism in our church. Perhaps we have done so and have found few, if any, standing with us, and we are about ready to give up our belief in the fundamentals of the Word of God. Do not give up. God is still in control of this world and this universe.

Perhaps we have tried hard to live for the Lord and have failed. Perhaps we failed today as we failed yesterday and the day before and are asking, "What's the use?" Let us come out of the cave of darkness and listen to the still, small voice of God. He tells us that He has given us all that pertains to life and godliness (II Pet. 1:3). Every provision has been made for us.

Again Peter speaks to us: "Wherefore the rather, brethren, give diligence to make your calling and election sure: for if ye do these things, ye shall never fall" (v. 10). The word "calling" refers to the fact that God has called us out of this world of sin and provided for us everything necessary to live a holy, godly life just as we read in verse 3. We are called out from human ways and from the rules and regulations of man-made systems to live our life in Christ. The fact that God has called us means that He has invited us to share His nature and power and everything that He wishes us to have.

In fact, God has promised to come and live His life in us so that He is our strength, the One who enables us to live a moral life. This is our calling, and we need to confirm it in our lives. We need to apply it by faith. To "make it sure" does not mean we put it into a place for safekeeping or put a padlock on it. It simply means that we accept it and act upon it because God has provided it.

The word "election" is based on the sovereign will of God and on the power and the purpose of God. The same truth is seen where we are told that we have been chosen in Him. God, for example, chose Abraham from all the rest of the people in Chaldea. It was not because Abraham was good in himself but because God decided Abraham was the man He wanted. The same Lord chose Isaac instead of Ishmael and Jacob instead of Esau. He has chosen us also for a special work, and He wants to see it fulfilled in us.

This was what Elijah found concerning his service. He found he was chosen to be the voice of thunder and of fire and of condemnation to Israel. This is what God had chosen him to be, and though the prophet would not see the fruit of it in his time, nevertheless, fruit would eventually come from it.

Because he knew that he had been called to a certain work and that he could not perform that work in himself, Paul said, "That I may know him [Christ], and the power of his resurrection" (Phil. 3:10). Paul wanted the Lord to live His life in him. That was why he decided to forget the things that were behind. He wanted to lay hold of that for which Christ had laid hold of him. So he reached out to those things that were ahead and pressed on toward the mark for the prize of the high calling of God in Christ Jesus (see vv. 12,13). He saw this calling as an invitation to accept Christ as his very life, a life to be lived in him anew and afresh from day to day.

Elijah Recommissioned

When God spoke in the still, small voice to Elijah, the prophet's heart broke. The God of Israel asked this man to let Him be his life. He said that He had chosen him to be His voice of thunder and not to be concerned about the fruit. That was God's business.

When Elijah recognized the grace of God, he hid his face. But he listened to the Lord when He said, "Go, return on thy way to the wilderness of Damascus: and when thou comest, anoint Hazael to be king over Syria" (I Kings 19:15). This man was going to be a rod to chastise Israel, and Elijah was to inaugurate this work.

He was also to anoint "Jehu the son of Nimshi" to be king over Israel (v. 16). What Hazael left, Jehu was to finish.

The third part of the commission was that Elijah was to anoint Elisha the son of Shaphat to be a prophet in his place. Elijah's work was not yet finished, but God had chosen a particular person to be his understudy and to carry on the work that he began.

Laborers Together

The fact that no one sees all the plan of God and no one sees all the fruit of his labors for God in his lifetime is taught very clearly in Hebrews 11. In verses 37-39, the writer said concerning the great heroes of the faith, "They were stoned, they were sawn asunder, were tempted, were slain with the sword: they wandered about in sheepskins and goatskins; being destitute, afflicted, tormented; (of whom the world was not worthy:) they wandered in deserts, and in mountains, and in dens and caves of the earth. And these all, having obtained a good report through faith, received not the promise." Though they were all faithful and true to the Lord, they did not see the complete results of their labors in their lifetime. The record continues: "God having provided some better thing for us, that they without us should not be made perfect" (v. 40). It takes all of God's people from the beginning of time to the very end to fulfill all that He has planned.

Over a period of years God adds this member and that member to do a particular task. This should keep us from discouragement when we fail to see fruit to any great extent in our lifetime. It may be fruit for which we have labored hard and long, but because we see little of it we think God has not worked through us.

If we are in the will of God, He is working through us. We need to recognize that we do one particular task, but we see the fruit by faith but not necessarily by sight. This is what the men of faith did, according to Hebrews 11. They did not see the fruit in their generation, but they did see it through faith. Like them we need to learn to fit into God's plan for us, and we will find that He is coordinating the work of all His children into one great master plan.

As we have noted before, Elijah was not consciously running from God, neither was he bitter. He was disappointed and depressed because he saw no national revival among the Israelites. He did not see the future as God saw it. Others would reap where he had sown.

How true that is in the experience of many today. Pastors labor hard in seeking to win the lost for Christ and perhaps see little fruit. Then an evangelist is called in, and he reaps the harvest and often the credit. Paul said that one plants, another waters, but God gives the increase (see I Cor. 3:6,7). He is also keeping the books and will give the rewards properly and justly (see v. 8).

This is true with regard to our work also. We do not see a great deal of the fruit that results from our preaching, but we do see some. Moreover, we rejoice when those who are saved through Back to the Bible's ministry join local churches where the Bible is taught and develop and grow under a local ministry. It takes many hands to do the work of the Lord.

Once Elijah was restored to fellowship with the Lord, he was recommissioned and told, "Go, return on thy way to the wilderness of Damascus" (I Kings 19:15). Elijah had to go back the way he had come to fulfill this commission. He had a long journey ahead of him.

This is the procedure that must be followed by anyone who has temporarily stepped out of the direct will of God. They must go back to the place where God's will can be followed once more.

For example, according to Genesis 12, Abraham was instructed to dwell in the land of Canaan, but when a famine struck, he went to Egypt. He stepped out of the direct will of God in doing this and found himself in deep trouble with Pharaoh. The Lord delivered him and sent him back to the land of promise; so Abraham "went on his journeys from the south even to Beth-el, unto the place where his tent had been at the beginning, between Beth-el and Hai; unto the place of the altar, which he had made there at the first: and there Abram called on the name of the Lord" (13:3,4).

Abraham lapsed in faith again at Gerar and had to be recalled from that place into the direct will of God. He had no fellowship with the Lord as long as he was away from the place God had designated as his dwelling place.

Abraham's grandson Jacob went through the same kind of experience. Because of some things he did he had to flee from the home of his parents and was away from the land for many years. Then God called him back to Bethel, but Jacob stayed at Shechem, where some very sad experiences took place. Then again God called him to go to Bethel and dwell there "and make there an altar unto God, that appeared unto thee when thou fleddest from the face of Esau thy brother. Then Jacob said unto his household, and to all that were with him, Put away the strange gods that are among you, and be clean, and change your garments: and let us arise, and go up to Beth-el; and I will make there an altar unto God, who answered me in the day of my distress" (35:1-3). He had to go back to the place where he left the revealed will of God before he could make a fresh start.

The same principle is taught in the Book of the Revelation. To the Church at Ephesus our Saviour said, "Nevertheless I have somewhat against thee, because thou hast left thy first love. Remember therefore from whence thou art fallen, and repent [turn around], and do the first works; or else I will come unto thee quickly, and will remove thy candlestick out of his place, except thou repent" (2:4,5).

Peter had to retrace his steps after he denied the Lord and before he was recommissioned. The Prodigal Son had to return from the far country to his father's house. He had to retrace his steps. This is not always easy to do.

Elijah's journey would take him back through the desert, on through Jezebel's homeland and all the way to Damascus. Had he stayed at Carmel and been given the instructions he was given while at Mount Horeb, he would have had only about 100 miles to go to Damascus. Added to that was now the distance from Mount Horeb.

The Word says, "He that covereth his sins shall not prosper: but whoso confesseth and forsaketh them [leaves them and returns to the Lord] shall have mercy" (Prov. 28:13).

Part of Elijah's recommissioning was to anoint Hazael king over Syria. This man was to be God's rod of chastisement on Israel. This anointing was not performed by Elijah, but by Elisha, who was Elijah's understudy. And when this prophet stood before Hazael, he wept. When asked why, he replied, "Because I know the evil that thou wilt do unto the children of Israel: their strong holds wilt thou set on fire, and their young men wilt thou slay with the sword, and wilt dash their children, and rip up their women with child" (II Kings 8:12). Hazael was like a tornado wherever he went. He represented the storm and the destruction of the fierce winds. This was the answer to Elijah's complaint about Israel's backsliding.

He was also to anoint Jehu, who was to bring judgment on the house of Ahab. This anointing was also not done directly by Elijah but by Elisha. Jehu was like an earthquake, shaking the house of Ahab from within. Jezebel was thrown down from a window of her home, and her body was eaten by dogs (9:30-37). Jehu killed 70 sons of Ahab in one day and made a public display of their heads (10:1-10). He also eradicated Baal worship. This was the answer of God to Elijah's complaint concerning the worship of Baal and the household of Ahab.

The third part of his commission was to anoint Elisha to take his place. This speaks of the power of the Word that was like a two-edged sword. This was an answer to Elijah's complaint that no prophet of Jehovah was left. The fire Elijah had kindled would continue through the ministry of Elisha.

God uses various instruments to do His work. Hazael, the king of Syria, brought ruthless judgment upon Israel. Jehu became a scourge to the house of Ahab and to the followers of Baal. Elisha, by his use of the Word of God and the power of God, slew the enemies of the Lord and comforted His people.

God sometimes uses wicked men to discipline His own children, but when these men overstep the boundaries God has set for them, judgment falls on their heads also.

God also reminded Elijah that there were 7000 persons left who had not bowed to Baal. This was all in God's dealing through the still, small voice of grace. It brought comfort to the prophet's heart. It assured him that the good work he had begun would be consummated under the hand of God and in God's time. Elijah did not see the fruit in his day, but he was promised a fruitful harvest for the future.

Chapter 11

The Call of Elisha

We must introduce Elisha into Elijah's life at this time in order to show how God works first through one man and then through another. This does not mean that God works in the same way through each one, but He uses each person in a particular way. We have already learned that Elijah was commissioned to anoint Elisha to take his place. Contrary to Elijah's belief, there were 7000 who had not bowed their knee to Baal. A literal translation of what God said to him is "I will keep me seven thousand, those who have not bowed their knee to Baal, or whose mouth has not kissed him" (I Kings 19:18). Elisha was of this number, and God directed his call and anointing for just the right time in Elijah's life and program.

Elijah was also to anoint Hazael to be king of Syria and Jehu to be king over Israel. Elijah actually performed only one of these anointings. The two kings were anointed by Elisha when he took over Elijah's ministry.

The outstanding factor concerning the older prophet's life was his obedience to God. He left Horeb to do God's will.

Like him, if we are going to be in God's work and have His blessing, we must be obedient. Men such as D. L. Moody were used because they were obedient. The great evangelist's life verse was one that spoke of obedience. He determined he would be obedient to God regardless of what God told him to do.

It does not matter whether or not people understand us or think we are even sane as long as we are true to God. Obedience to Him is the important thing.

The meaning of these two men's names is instructive. Elijah means "my God is Jehovah." Elisha, on the other hand, means "God his salvation." Just as the names meant different things though both men honored God, so their life work differed though they both served God.

Elijah was like Moses in that he vindicated the divine holiness of God. He was an ambassador of wrath against lawlessness and rebellion. Elisha was an evangelist, a representative of God's loving-kindness. The main thrust of his ministry was not to threaten or terrify but to persuade and to convert people. Both men received their message from God, but the messages differed. This was God ordained. Some are called of God to give a message of condemnation and of judgment while others speak more of God's grace. The Holy Spirit has absolute sovereignty in giving gifts and in choosing whom He will to perform specific tasks.

We learn from I Corinthians 12: "Now there are diversities of gifts, but the same Spirit. And there are differences of administrations, but the same Lord [different ways things can be done under the direction of the same Spirit]. And there are diversities of operations, but it is the same God which worketh all in all. But the manifestation of the Spirit is given to every man to profit withal. . . . But all these worketh that one and the selfsame Spirit, dividing to every man severally as he will" (vv. 4-7,11).

This whole chapter in I Corinthians shows that the Body of Christ is like a human body with many members. No two members have the same task. Our responsibility is to fulfill the task given us by God and not to try to imitate someone else.

Elisha's Background

Elijah found Elisha plowing in a field along with his servants. There were 12 yoke of oxen, 12 plows and 11 servants. Elisha was in charge of the last plow. This indicates that he was not farming just a small piece of land but had a large farm.

135

The fact that he was with the 12th yoke of oxen shows that he did not feel that he was too important as the proprietor of a large farm to work alongside his servants. He was apparently a humble man, and this reminds us that God, according to I Corinthians 1:26, does not call many mighty to do His work.

Elisha was not proud; he was the last man in line, humble enough to be in the last row following the plow.

When Elijah found him, he "cast his mantle upon him" (I Kings 19:19). The prophet did not have a long talk with him and discuss the various aspects of the work involved. By casting his cloak over Elisha, he was simply saying to him that he was God's chosen man and that he was to follow Elijah. Elisha understood quite well what was meant.

God exercises the same sovereign right in our lives. He chooses whom He will. In John 15:16 the Lord Jesus said, "Ye have not chosen me, but I have chosen you, and ordained you, that ye should go and bring forth fruit, and that your fruit should remain: that whatsoever ye shall ask of the Father in my name, he may give it you."

The Apostle Paul wrote about this same matter in II Corinthians 5: "And all things are of God, who hath reconciled us to himself by Jesus Christ, and hath given to us the ministry of reconciliation; to wit, that God was in Christ, reconciling the world unto himself" (vv. 18,19). This refers to service. The choice is not ours; it belongs to God.

Elisha's Response

Elisha apparently decided immediately to go with Elijah. It was a dangerous matter in that day for anyone to make it known that he was going to follow the Lord. Jezebel's vindictive and cruel spirit was still being manifested, and anyone declaring himself to be a prophet of God would be in danger of losing his life. Elijah, of course, had been spared, and Elisha did not hesitate when he was commissioned.

He immediately left his oxen, ran after Elijah and said he would like to stay behind a little while to make a feast and say good-bye to his friends and his parents.

I believe he planned a public farewell as a witness to his family and his friends. This was different from the account recorded in the New Testament of the person who was asked to follow the Lord but requested that he might go back and bury his father. He meant, of course, that he wanted to stay at home until his father died. He wanted to take care of that family responsibility before he followed the Lord. The Lord Jesus said, "Let the dead bury their dead" (Matt. 8:22).

Elisha, however, did not say, "Let me bury my parents" but rather "Let me kiss them good-bye." This was an entirely different situation.

A great New Testament principle concerning this is given in Luke 14:25-27: "And there went great multitudes with him: and he turned, and said unto them, If any man come to me, and hate not his father, and mother, and wife, and children, and brethren, and sisters, yea, and his own life also, he cannot be my disciple. And whosoever doth not bear his cross, and come after me, cannot be my disciple." The word "hate" in this passage is not used in a bad sense. Our Saviour was simply saying that the person who does not put his family in second place and Christ in first place cannot be His disciple. We must love the Lord supremely; if we do, we will put even our closest loved ones in a secondary position.

Elijah's answer was "Go back again: for what have I done to thee?" (I Kings 19:20). I believe Elijah was saying to Elisha that he should settle the matter with God, not with him. Many times we feel we have to make excuses to people, but when we are right with God, we do not have to justify ourselves before others. I think that is what Elijah was saying to Elisha. God was choosing Elisha; so whatever Elisha did about it was to be settled with God and not with Elijah.

Elisha made a complete break with his past. He made a complete surrender to God and broke off all ties with his old life. He took the yoke of oxen he had been plowing with — possibly his best — and killed them for the dual purpose of making an offering to God and giving a feast for his friends. He used the plow and the yokes as firewood. Thus, he made a complete sacrifice. His friends and neighbors saw him burning all his bridges behind him, cutting off all connections with his former life and property.

Romans 12:1 says, "I beseech you therefore, brethren, by the mercies of God, that ye present your bodies a living sacrifice, holy, acceptable unto God, which is your reasonable service." Everything we have, according to this, belongs to God. Sacrifice usually involves death, but this passage speaks of a living sacrifice — we are to give ourselves to God to live entirely for Him. If we are to be true servants of the Lord, this is the kind of sacrifice involved.

After Elisha had provided a feast for the people and kissed his parents good-bye, he arose and followed Elijah. The older prophet became his spiritual teacher, and Elisha took the humble place of being his servant. He served a man in serving God. This is what Joshua did with regard to Moses, and then God called him to lead the people after Moses' death. This is the method God sometimes uses in giving men their basic training for His service. This is not the only method He uses, but this is the one He used in Elisha's case.

Chapter 12

Elijah Announces Ahab's Doom

Following the appointment of Elisha, five or six years passed before Elijah's ministry was again public. He was not inactive during this period but seems to have been forming schools of the prophets, schools in which the Bible was taught to young men who were in turn to be instructors and teachers of the Word of God. Elijah was a spiritual father and the teacher of many of these young servants of God.

During this same time, great wars occurred between Israel and Syria. Ahab took an active part in these, and from time to time prophets of lesser stature than that of Elijah appeared briefly on the scene.

Then one day God again told Elijah to appear before Ahab to announce that monarch's doom. This was due to a very wicked crime he had committed.

A Terrible Deed

In the city of Jezreel, near the palace of Ahab, was a vineyard owned by Naboth. The king wanted this vineyard for himself and asked Naboth to sell it. Naboth, who was a God-fearing man, stated that he was forbidden of the Lord to sell the vineyard, for it was his inheritance from his fathers.

Ahab acted like a spoiled child when he returned to his palace. He went to bed and turned his face away from his servants and refused to eat.

When Jezebel, his wife, learned of his sulking and child-ish behavior, she questioned him to find out its cause. Her cruel mind soon devised a solution, and she told her husband to arise and be cheerful, for the vineyard was as good as his. She put her plan into action. Through forged letters and false witnesses and a trial that was a mockery, she had Naboth put to death with the sanction of law. Apparently his sons were also murdered at this time, though we are not given the details concerning their deaths (II Kings 9:26).

Though the scheme was Jezebel's, the guilt was shared by her weak and pouting husband. He had little time to go to Naboth's vineyard and gloat over his new possession before Elijah stood before him. Faithful to the trust committed to him by God, Elijah wasted no time in presenting himself before the king. Ahab's first words to him were "Hast thou found me, O mine enemy?" (I Kings 21:20).

The prophet replied, "I have found thee: because thou hast sold thyself to work evil in the sight of the Lord" (v. 20). Jezebel and Ahab may have thought they had covered up their crime quite well, but God had seen what they had done. Nothing was hidden from God's eyes. He neither slumbers nor sleeps (see Ps. 121:4). All things are open before Him (see Heb. 4:13).

John's description of the Lord Jesus Christ in the Book of the Revelation adds force to this fact. "His eyes were as a flame of fire; and his feet like unto fine brass, as if they burned in a furnace; and his voice as the sound of many waters" (1:14,15). His eyes see all. Nothing can be hidden from Him. The darkness is like daylight to Him (see Ps. 139:12). His eyes are eyes of fire.

God is never mocked. Whatever a man sows, he reaps (Gal. 6:7,8). Ahab should have remembered that his sin would find him out (see Num. 32:23). Naboth lay buried under the earth, but the voice of his blood cried to heaven for vengeance. People may get away with murder before others, but they never get away with anything before God. We read: "For we know him that hath said, Vengeance belongeth unto me, I will recompense, saith the Lord. And again, The Lord shall judge his people. It is a fearful thing to fall into the hands of the living God" (Heb. 10:30,31).

We should never think we can get by with sin. "The eyes of the Lord are in every place, beholding the evil and the good" (Prov. 15:3). A day of reckoning is coming, and God is keeping the record of all events. He does not keep books because He forgets but as written evidence to convince any of us who might dispute the truth.

Jeremiah stated, "Can any hide himself in secret places that I shall not see him? saith the Lord. Do not I fill heaven and earth? saith the Lord" (Jer. 23:24). In Job we read: "For his eyes are upon the ways of man, and he seeth all his goings. There is no darkness, nor shadow of death, where the workers of iniquity may hide themselves" (34:21,22). We can hide nothing from the eyes of God.

God always denounces sin. Ahab soon learned of God's displeasure and anger at this terrible deed. God's warnings today are just as clear and definite. To those so-called ministers who do not preach the Gospel, Jeremiah said, "Behold, a whirlwind of the Lord is gone forth in fury, even a grievous whirlwind: it shall fall grievously upon the head of the wicked" (Jer. 23:19). A whirlwind is like a tornado. It is destructive. The prophet continued, "The anger of the Lord shall not return, until he have executed, and till he have performed the thoughts of his heart: in the latter days ye shall consider it perfectly. I have not sent these prophets, yet they ran: I have not spoken to them, yet they prophesied. . . . I have heard what the prophets said, that prophesy lies in my name, saying, I have dreamed, I have dreamed" (vv. 20,21,25).

Still speaking out against these prophets, the Lord said through Jeremiah: "Is not my word like as a fire? saith the Lord; and like a hammer that breaketh the rock in pieces? Therefore, behold, I am against the prophets, saith the Lord, that steal my words every one from his neighbour. Behold, I am against the prophets, saith the Lord, that use their tongues, and say, He saith" (vv. 29-31).

False prophets today deny that Jesus Christ is the eternal God and that He came and died for our sins. They also deny that it is necessary for people to be born again. They try to tickle the ears of their hearers with teachings that are not from God. God said concerning them, "I have not sent them, and I am coming like a whirlwind to judge them."

We can all be sure that our sins will find us out. Adam thought he could hide from God, but God found him. Cain murdered Abel, but Abel's blood cried to God from the ground. Achan stole the accursed thing, but God knew it. Ahab, who was jointly responsible with his wife for the murder of Naboth, could not escape the eye of God. God found him out. Gehazi, the servant of Elisha, thought he could do something behind Elisha's back that would increase his personal wealth, but God saw his sin and denounced him through the prophet. Ananias and Sapphira thought they could lie to God and He would not see through it, but they were wrong. Let no one think he can escape divine retribution for wrong done.

The Scriptures are very clear on this. In Jude 1:14,15, we learn: "Behold, the Lord cometh with ten thousands of his saints, to execute judgment upon all, and to convince all that are ungodly among them of all their ungodly deeds which they have ungodly committed, and of all their hard speeches which ungodly sinners have spoken against him."

Ahab sold himself to work evil in the sight of the Lord, but he could not get away with it. The Bible declares, "All have sinned, and come short of the glory of God" (Rom. 3:23). It also states, "The wages of sin is death; but the gift of God is eternal life through Jesus Christ" (6:23). Those who, like Ahab, sell themselves to work evil in the sight of God will be found out. It is true that mercy belongs to God, but mercy cannot be earned. We cannot merit it. The wages of sin is death. It is only through the gift of God that we can receive eternal life through Jesus Christ our Lord.

I have known Christians who have sold themselves to sin, even some Christian leaders, but the Lord warns us: "Know ye not that ye are the temple of God, and that the Spirit of God dwelleth in you? If any man defile the temple of God, him shall God destroy; for the temple of God is holy, which temple ye are" (I Cor. 3:16,17).

Let us not think we have time on our hands to make things right with God. Today is the day of salvation. Or if you are already saved but need to return to fellowship, now is the time to come back to the Lord. Do not wait until tomorrow.

> I may not see
> The rising of the sun.
> When evening falls
> My work all may be done.
> So today is mine—
> Tomorrow may not come.

The Judgments of God

Because Ahab had sold himself to do evil, God said through Elijah that He would bring evil upon him and upon his posterity and would cut off all the male members of his household (I Kings 21:21). Concerning Jezebel, God said, "The dogs shall eat Jezebel by the wall of Jezreel. Him that dieth of Ahab in the city the dogs shall eat; and him that dieth in the field shall the fowls of the air eat" (vv. 23,24).

Ahab postponed his own death through partial repentance. We are told that "he rent his clothes, and put sackcloth upon his flesh, and fasted, and lay in sackcloth, and went softly" (v. 27). Because of this the Lord said, "I will not bring the evil in his days: but in his son's days will I bring the evil upon his house" (v. 29).

Ahab's death was, nonetheless, a violent death. Three years later he was severely wounded in battle and died as a result. "And a certain man drew a bow at a venture, and smote the king of Israel between the joints of the harness: wherefore he said unto the driver of his chariot, Turn thine hand, and carry me out of the host; for I am wounded. And the battle increased that day: and the king . . . died at even: and the blood ran out of the wound into the midst of the chariot. . . . So the king died, and was brought to Samaria; and they buried the king in Samaria. And one washed the chariot in the pool of Samaria; and dogs licked up his blood;

and they washed his armour; according unto the word of the Lord which he spake" (22:34,35,37,38).

Several years later, when Jehu came to Jezreel, divine retribution fell on Jezebel. Apparently Jezebel thought that her beauty was sufficient to beguile Jehu; so she "painted her face, and tired her head, and looked out at a window" (II Kings 9:30). He would not listen to her and had some of her eunuchs throw her out of her window. "So they threw her down: and some of her blood was sprinkled on the wall, and on the horses: and he trode her under foot" (v. 33).

After he had eaten, the thought occurred to him that Jezebel was a king's daughter and ought to be treated with a certain degree of respect; so he sent men to bury her, but they found nothing more than the skull and the feet and the palms of her hands. When his servants brought him word, he said, "This is the word of the Lord, which he spake by his servant Elijah the Tishbite, saying, In the portion of Jezreel shall dogs eat the flesh of Jezebel: and the carcase of Jezebel shall be as dung upon the face of the field in the portion of Jezreel; so that they shall not say, This is Jezebel" (vv. 36,37).

This was a fearful judgment, but she was an unrepentant rebel against God. She introduced Baal worship into the palace and into the kingdom although she had every evidence that God was God. She knew of the miracles performed by Elijah. She reaped what she had sown.

Second Kings 10 tells how Ahab's family was destroyed: "And it came to pass . . . that they took the king's sons, and slew seventy persons, and put their heads in baskets, and sent him them to Jezreel. And there came a messenger, and told him [Jehu], saying, They have brought the heads of the king's sons. And he said, Lay ye them in two heaps at the entering in of the gate until the morning. And it came to pass in the morning, that he went out, and stood, and said to all the people, Ye be righteous: behold, I conspired against my master, and slew him: but who slew all these? Know now that there shall fall unto the earth nothing of the word of the Lord, which the Lord spake concerning the house of Ahab: for the Lord hath done that which he spake by his servant

Elijah. So Jehu slew all that remained of the house of Ahab in Jezreel, and all his great men, and his kinsfolks, and his priests, until he left him none remaining" (vv. 7-11).

Just before slaying Jezebel, Jehu had put to death Joram, Ahab's son, who was then king of Israel. Joram had been wounded in a battle with the Syrians and was recuperating from his wounds in Jezreel when Jehu came to the city.

Joram's first words were "Is it peace, Jehu?" (II Kings 9:22).

He answered, "What peace, so long as the whoredoms of thy mother Jezebel and her witchcrafts are so many?" (v. 22).

At this Joram fled, but Jehu drew a bow "with his full strength, and smote Jehoram [Joram] between his arms, and the arrow went out at his heart, and he sunk down in his chariot. Then said Jehu to Bidkar his captain, Take up, and cast him in the portion of the field of Naboth the Jezreelite: for remember how that, when I and thou rode together after Ahab his father, the Lord laid this burden upon him; surely I have seen yesterday the blood of Naboth, and the blood of his sons, saith the Lord; and I will requite thee in this plat, saith the Lord. Now therefore take and cast him into the plat of ground, according to the word of the Lord" (vv. 24-26). So Joram the son of Ahab not only met a violent death, but also he was buried in the very field his father had murdered Naboth for.

God's judgments are sure. "It is appointed unto men once to die, but after this the judgment" (Heb. 9:27). We cannot get away from it. God said it, and that settles it. Another warning in Hebrews is "How shall we escape, if we neglect so great salvation?" (2:3). This was spoken to those who were already believers but who did not want to go on to maturity in Christ. Some of us accept salvation from sin's guilt and condemnation but do not allow the living Christ to be our Lord. "How shall we escape, if we neglect so great salvation?"

We considered previously that Ahab showed repentance when Elijah pronounced God's judgment on him. The king was terror stricken because he knew that the words of the prophet would come true. Elijah's word to him was God speaking to him.

Ahab's sin was threefold. First, he provoked the anger of God by sinning against Him. Then he made Israel sin. And third, he sold himself to work wickedness.

God's judgment will be severe against men such as Ahab who not only deny the truth themselves but also lead others down the same corrupt path. Peter warned concerning this: "But there were false prophets also among the people, even as there shall be false teachers among you, who privily shall bring in damnable heresies, even denying the Lord that bought them and bring upon themselves swift destruction" (II Pet. 2:1). There is such preaching in so-called Christian pulpits today, and "many shall follow their pernicious ways; by reason of whom the way of truth shall be evil spoken of. And through covetousness shall they with feigned words make merchandise of you: whose judgment now of a long time lingereth not, and their damnation [judgment] slumbereth not" (vv. 2,3).

The Lord said no one was like Ahab, who sold himself to work wickedness in the sight of the Lord and who was stirred up by Jezebel his wife (I Kings 21:25). This was an evil combination and showed that Ahab had his price. There is a saying, "Every man has his price." This is not true with regard to the man who is truly committed to God.

What price will we sell ourselves for? Will it be material gain? Even some Christians are willing to compromise to gain the riches of this world.

The price for other unbelievers and God's people alike is the price of honor, of profit or of pleasure. Ahab sold himself for his affection for Jezebel. However, he was not so set in sin that he could not or would not take a warning seriously. When Elijah pronounced judgment on him, he forgot his pride and his crown and humbled himself for a while. But his repentance was one of fear, not of love. It was not genuine.

First, true repentance causes us to see that our sins are against God and His love. Second, we see ourselves condemned and guilty, and so we plead before God. Third, true repentance also reviews the mercies of God, which are seen in Christ Jesus, His Son. In the fourth place, we accept God's provision of salvation in Christ, who died for our sins. Then, in the fifth place, we run from sin as from a serpent, not because we fear the consequences but because we love Christ. Finally, we present ourselves to God so that He might truly possess us and use us to His own honor and glory. Ahab's repentance was not of this nature. Fear of the punishment, not the awfulness of his sin, caused him to tremble. Had no curse been placed on him, his sins and evil ways would have pained him very little. Yet even this humbling of himself, though it was only partial repentance, brought a delay of judgment. How merciful is our God!

Elijah's Last Task

Before tragedy finally destroyed the last of Ahab's family, an incident recorded in II Kings 1 gives us insight into the character of Ahab's children and the record of the last public act of the Prophet Elijah.

Following Ahab as king was Ahaziah his son. His rule was very brief, and his death is an illustration of God's judgment on rebels who persist in defying God. Ahaziah was the playboy type who enjoyed the privileges of rulership but wanted nothing to do with its responsibilities. Moab rebelled against Israel after the death of Ahab, and Ahaziah could not care less. His attitude was to let Moab rebel. It mattered nothing to him.

This brief bit of history about Ahaziah begins with his falling through a lattice work in his upper chamber in Samaria. The fall was apparently severe, for he was very ill and wondered if he would recover. He sent messengers with these instructions: "Go, enquire of Baal-zebub the god of Ekron whether I shall recover of this disease" (v. 2). Baal-zebub was the name under which Baal was worshiped by the Philistines. He was the god of medicine and also the god of the flies. This, of course, was the same demon worship that had brought disaster on Ahab and Israel.

Nothing is hidden from God, and the angel of the Lord "said to Elijah the Tishbite, Arise, go up to meet the messengers of the king of Samaria, and say unto them, Is it not because there is not a God in Israel, that ye go to enquire of Baal-zebub the god of Ekron? Now therefore thus saith the Lord, Thou shalt not come down from that bed on which thou art gone up, but shalt surely die" (vv. 3,4). Elijah immediately departed after delivering this message. This was the last task God gave him. Just as the prophet had been sent to rebuke Ahab, now he was sent to rebuke Ahab's son.

The messengers turned around and went back to the king, who was surprised to see them so soon. He said to them, "Why are ye now turned back?" (v. 5).

"And they said unto him, There came a man up to meet us, and said unto us, Go, turn again unto the king that sent you, and say unto him, Thus saith the Lord, Is it not because there is not a God in Israel, that thou sendest to enquire of Baal–zebub the god of Ekron? therefore thou shalt not come down from that bed on which thou art gone up, but shalt surely die" (v. 6).

Ahaziah then asked them, "What manner of man was he which came up to meet you, and told you these words?" (v. 7).

They answered, "He was an hairy man, and girt with a girdle of leather about his loins" (v. 8).

The king immediately identified the man as Elijah the Tishbite. He was not ignorant of the part Elijah had played in the history of Ahab and Israel, but in spite of his knowledge, this new king was worse than his father. He sent a captain and 50 soldiers to take Elijah prisoner. This was an open challenge against God Himself. Ahaziah was so proud that he thought he could fight against God by fighting God's man.

Do we realize that this will take place again and on a much greater scale? The Battle of Armageddon will be nothing less than the Satan-inspired Antichrist's rousing his followers to fight against the armies of heaven. They will actually believe they can win the contest, but they will not. Satan always sends his followers to their doom. Someone reading these words may even be playing into the hands of the Devil himself. Satan will not be able to rescue anyone from the judgment of God. In spite of his promises, Satan can guarantee only the wages of sin, and they are death.

Evil people will not face the facts of God's judgment. Ahaziah would not and struck out against the person who dared to proclaim God's message. It seems to be a human trait to think that we can do away with God's judgment by striking down God's messenger. How false this idea is, for God will not be mocked. A person will reap whatever he sows (Gal. 6:7). God is a consuming fire (see Heb. 12:29). It is a fearful thing to face His judgment (see 10:31).

When people turn from God's truth as proclaimed in His Word, they are not only rejecting God's messengers, but also they are rejecting God Himself. Their rebellion is not against men but against God. They will have to face Him someday. How can they expect to stand in such a judgment?

The soldiers found Elijah on the top of a hill. It might have been Mount Carmel where he witnessed God's great triumph in sending fire to consume the offering on the altar. Perhaps Elijah had gone to this hill, wherever it was, to pray and to fellowship with God. Moses followed this practice, and so did the Lord Jesus during his public ministry. The practice speaks of isolation and seclusion — the servant's being alone with God.

Judgment by Fire

The captain said to Elijah, "Thou man of God, the king hath said, Come down" (II Kings 1:9). The captain may have called Elijah a man of God in mockery, but God cannot be mocked. Elijah sat in safety, for as God's representative, he had nothing to fear.

He answered the jibe in these words: "And Elijah answered and said to the captain of fifty, If I be a man of God, then let fire come down from heaven, and consume thee and thy fifty" (v. 10). God vindicated His servant, and fire fell from heaven and consumed the captain and his men.

On Mount Carmel the fire had fallen and consumed the sacrifice while the people went free. The prophets of Baal, of course, were an exception, for they had sold themselves to sin.

On Mount Calvary, God's wrath fell on His Son, who died in our place that we might go free. All God asks is that we accept Christ as our Saviour, trusting Him to save us from sin. But those who refuse, those who will not turn to God, will not find the rest God gives His people. Instead, they will be judged: "And to you who are troubled rest with us, when the Lord Jesus shall be revealed from heaven with his mighty angels, in flaming fire taking vengeance on them that know not [ignore] God, and obey not the gospel of our Lord Jesus Christ: who shall be punished with everlasting destruction from the presence of the Lord, and from the glory of his power" (II Thess. 1:7-9).

These soldiers came without repentant hearts and without a sacrifice, and so they faced the judgment of their own sin. They did not turn to God. The warning in the Scripture is "Without shedding of blood is no remission [of sin]" (Heb. 9:22). The Bible also warns, "It is a fearful thing to fall into the hands of the living God" (10:31).

Elijah's calling down fire on these men was not the result of personal revenge on his part. He was a true servant of God and reflected the heart of God, who finds no pleasure in the death of the wicked. God is "longsuffering to us-ward, not willing that any should perish, but that all should come to repentance" (II Pet. 3:9).

The king learned nothing from the loss of these men and sent out a second captain with 50 soldiers. Perhaps Ahaziah and some of the others thought that an accident had taken place. They may have thought the death of these men was caused by lightning and was not the result of God's direct judgment. But they ignored the evidence that was startling and clear. The bodies of the slain men were mute testimony to what had taken place. Elijah answered the second captain as he had the first, and fire came down from heaven and consumed them (II Kings 1:12).

One wonders how blind and calloused a man can become! Ahaziah had sent more than 100 men to their death; yet he sent a third group with the same instructions — to bring Elijah in.

The captain of this third 50 was different from the others. He "came and fell on his knees before Elijah, and besought him, and said unto him, O man of God, I pray thee, let my life, and the life of these fifty thy servants, be precious in thy sight. Behold, there came fire down from heaven, and burnt up the two captains of the former fifties with their fifties: therefore let my life be now precious in thy sight" (vv.13,14).

This captain approached God's servant, showing reverence in his heart for God and pleading for mercy. He showed submission to the living God. This must have caused Elijah to rejoice, for, like God, he had no pleasure in the death of the wicked. Nevertheless, judgment has been sent by God on several occasions to warn the ungodly: "For if God spared not the angels that sinned, but cast them down to hell, and delivered them into chains of darkness, to be reserved unto judgment; and spared not the old world, but saved Noah the eighth person, a preacher of righteousness, bringing in the flood upon the world of the ungodly; and turning the cities of Sodom and Gomorrha into ashes condemned them with an overthrow, making them an ensample unto those that after should live ungodly" (II Pet. 2:4-6).

Elijah was assured by the angel of the Lord that no harm would come to him and that he was to go with the captain and give God's message to the king in person. Soon after this Ahaziah died, and Jehoram reigned in his place.

All who reject Jesus Christ will meet Him in person: "And I saw a great white throne, and him that sat on it, from whose face the earth and the heaven fled away; and there was found no place for them. And I saw the dead, small and great, stand before God; and the books were opened: and another book was opened, which is the book of life: and the dead were judged out of those things which were written in the books, according to their works. And the sea gave up the dead which were in it; and death and hell delivered up the dead which were in them: and they were judged every man according to their works. And death and hell were cast into the lake of fire. This is the second death. And whosoever was not found written in the book of life was cast into the lake of fire" (Rev. 20:11-15).

"Prepare to meet thy God" (Amos 4:12).

Chapter 13

Translation of Elijah

The closing incident in Elijah's life was perhaps the most touching in his whole history. He was translated to heaven without having to die. His ministry may have covered 15 or 20 years, but the public aspect of it was much briefer than that. At a time of great depression in his life, when lying under a juniper tree, he had prayed for death, but when the time of his translation came, he was thankful that God had not answered that prayer.

The prophet's translation was to be at a specially designated place. Elijah had learned long ago that absolute obedience to God's directions was necessary for God's blessings. Only at the Brook Cherith were the ravens instructed to bring food to him. Only in the city of Zarephath was there a widow with a little oil and meal who would sustain him. So Elijah knew how essential it was to be in the right place in order to see the fulfillment of God's promises.

The record of this great event is in II Kings 2. In verse 1 we are told that when the Lord was ready to take Elijah into heaven by a whirlwind, the prophet and his servant, Elisha, left Gilgal. He had been training young men, possibly some of the 7000 who had not bowed their knee to Baal. He had established three schools—one at Gilgal, one at Bethel and one at Jericho. This was not something new in Israel; Samuel had done this long before. Young prophets came out of these schools who were used by the Lord, men such as Amos.

Elijah began his journey from Gilgal to the place of his ascension, and Elisha insisted on going with him. This journey involved a great test for Elisha, who was to be Elijah's successor. From the account you may be led to think that Elijah was reluctant to have Elisha go with him, but this may well have been part of the test for the younger man. Elijah was alone in his ministry, and he was humble, and he may have felt that his coming translation was too sacred a matter to be witnessed by others.

We can learn valuable lessons from this experience. If we wish to behold the glory of God and to be fit vessels to participate in God's work, we must go on to maturity in Christ.

Gilgal

As we have already seen, Elijah's journey began at Gilgal. This place is noteworthy because one of Elijah's schools was there. This was the place where Elisha was first tested when he stated that he wanted to follow Elijah.

Second Kings 2:2 says, "And Elijah said unto Elisha, Tarry here [at Gilgal], I pray thee; for the Lord hath sent me to Beth-el. And Elisha said unto him, As the Lord liveth, and as thy soul liveth, I will not leave thee. So they went down to Beth-el."

Elisha was given the opportunity to stay at Gilgal, which seems to represent the easy, or comfortable, place for Christian living. It is not so hard to be a Christian — to be born again, to attend a good Bible-believing church on Sundays and to attend a prayer meeting during the week. Private, personal devotions are also beneficial and essential to the Christian life. These things are usually easy to do in a comfortable situation without the temptations of the Devil or the flesh. There is no call for any vital decisions, and there is little or no participation in spiritual warfare. We can go about our daily lives anticipating that the Lord will one day call us home to heaven where we can rejoice forever.

Bethel

Bethel speaks of something else again. The word itself means "house of God." This was where Jacob first met God when he fled from Esau. It was the place to which God called Jacob back after he had been with Laban for 20 years. It was the place of major decisions in Jacob's life, and he should have stayed closer to it.

Bethel speaks to us of a once-for-all decision that we as believers must make. The New Testament also refers to this: "I beseech you therefore, brethren, by the mercies of God, that ye present your bodies a living sacrifice, holy, acceptable unto God, which is your reasonable service" (Rom. 12:1). There comes a time in our Christian experience when we each have to face this decision.

We need to analyze this verse very carefully. It follows a portion in the Book of Romans in which God definitely outlined the marvelous plan for the Christian's life. It is to be a life of complete victory, a life of usefulness to God. Before this can be realized, God must have complete possession of us. This is seen in the phrase "present [yield] your bodies a living sacrifice." The Lord has purchased this body for His own possession (I Cor. 6:19,20). We are not our own; nevertheless, He does not force Himself upon us. He indwells us when we are born again, but we may give Him only part of our heart. He needs all of us, however, in order to live His life in us through Christ Jesus our Lord.

This is to be a once-for-all decision of yielding our bodies to God as living sacrifices. The word "sacrifice" itself speaks of death, and yet this is to be a living sacrifice that speaks of activity. This seeming paradox is explained by the fact that we are to die to self but to live unto God through an act of faith. This is taught in Romans 6:11 and is our reasonable service. Nothing is to be held back. Bethel speaks to us of this great choice.

Elijah said the Lord had sent him from Gilgal to Bethel. His had been a life of receiving direct orders from God and obeying them explicitly. How would Elisha measure up in these things? That was the test, but Elisha did not hesitate.

154

The expression "as the Lord liveth, and as thy soul liveth, I will not leave thee" (II Kings 2:2) may be restated, "As sure as God lives in you and in me, I will not leave you." This is an absolute and final statement. This is a choice from which there is no backing down.

Elisha made this decision willingly, and it is the kind of decision God requires of us. He never forces Himself on us. Once we decide to yield ourselves to God, there is no limit to what He can do through us. When we give our bodies to Him completely, we can say, as Paul did, "I can do all things through Christ which strengtheneth me" (Phil. 4:13).

Stating it from another angle, Paul said in Galatians 2:20, "The life which I now live in the flesh I live by the faith of the Son of God, who loved me, and gave himself for me."

Recognizing then that we must completely surrender to God, let us not stop at Gilgal, which represents a comfortable Christian life, but let us go on to Bethel, where He calls us to fully surrender to Him. He does not ask us all to be preachers or missionaries, but He does ask us to present our bodies so that He may indwell us completely in every aspect of our being.

Jericho

In II Kings 2:4 we read: "And Elijah said unto him, Elisha, tarry here, I pray thee; for the Lord hath sent me to Jericho." Elijah said, in effect, to Elisha that since he had decided to obey the Lord, he would not be staying at Bethel. He had come a long way in his spiritual life. So he could afford to stay for a while at Bethel, but that was not what Elisha decided to do. Again he said, "As the Lord liveth, and as thy soul liveth, I will not leave thee. So they came to Jericho" (v. 4).

Jericho represents the place of spiritual warfare — entering into activity against forces of evil for the Lord. This goes far beyond the average Christian's churchgoing and attending evangelistic campaigns — which are good — but this goes much further. This is the hardest phase of Christian living, but one we must enter if we would reap the greatest benefits in service and rewards. This is not something that is done in public but in private. There is no glamour to this aspect of the Christian life, but it results in effective service when entered into in the power of the Lord.

Three Steps in Israel's Deliverance

Looking at the three basic steps in Israel's deliverance from Egypt will help us see what is involved in this truth. First of all, when the Israelites were slaves in Egypt, they could do nothing to help themselves. God had to liberate them, and He did. The blood on the doorposts of the houses was the sign of their salvation. The manifestation of God's power at the Red Sea, which delivered them completely from Egypt and its armies, speaks of moving from death to life in God Himself. This was all God's doing. It represents our deliverance from the guilt and condemnation of sin and emancipation from the world. But what follows?

The second great experience for Israel was in the desert. There they were to learn to follow God completely so that they would be separated not only from a sinful world but also from a sinful self-life. One generation never did learn this, for all they did was complain. They went in circles, wandering in the desert for 40 years. This is true of a lot of believers who settle down in religious activities. They fail to go on to complete consecration and separation to the Lord or to enter into spiritual warfare. They follow a program of weekly church attendance, but they make no progress in their Christian lives because they have no purpose beyond attending meetings. This is no better than the Israelite's wandering in the wilderness and murmuring and traveling in circles. To do the former is right, but to fail to grow in the Christian life is sin. "Whatsoever is not of faith is sin" (Rom. 14:23).

The third great experience for the Israelites came when they crossed the Jordan. Then they came to Jericho and entered into warfare in order to possess the land. They were useless to God as far as their testimony was concerned while in Egypt and in the desert. Not until they came to the land itself could God work through them to possess it.

We are useless to God as long as we are in the world. We are also useless to Him as long as we merely follow a church program instead of getting out of the self-life and into the full life of separation and warfare represented by Canaan.

As soon as the Israelites entered the Promised Land, satanic opposition appeared. We can expect this also as soon as we enter into spiritual warfare. That is why Ephesians 6 was written. "Finally, my brethren, be strong in the Lord, and in the power of his might. Put on the whole armour of God, that ye may be able to stand against the wiles of the devil. For we wrestle not against flesh and blood, but against principalities, against powers, against the rulers of the darkness of this world, against spiritual wickedness in high places. Wherefore take unto you the whole armour of God, that ye may be able to withstand in the evil day, and having done all, to stand" (Eph. 6:10-13).

In this spiritual warfare God provides armor for our protection where necessary, and for offensive fighting, He furnishes us with the sword. Through faith we enter into this active service with Him, which is climaxed by warfare, through prayer. God needs more prayer warriors today among His people. Let us join this aggressive group.

Jordan

Elisha chose to go with Elijah to Jericho just as he had chosen to go with him to Bethel. But now their journey took them even farther. Elijah asked Elisha to stay at Jericho, for he said, "The Lord hath sent me to Jordan" (II Kings 2:6). Again Elisha refused and journeyed with his master. Jordan speaks of death. It represents death to the self-life. Jordan stands as the place of the Israelite's separation from the self-life in the desert to the life of warfare for the Lord in the land.

Have we passed through this in our daily experience? True, we have been born again and have been united to Christ. We have been identified with Him in His death, burial and resurrection. But not until we appropriate this by faith and enter into it actively in His name does it mean anything to us.

The cardinal chapter of the Bible for this subject is Romans 6. There we read: "Knowing this, that our old man is crucified with him, that the body of sin might be destroyed, that henceforth we should not serve sin" (v. 6). This speaks of the potential of the Christian life. But in order to actually enter it, here is what is needed: "Likewise reckon ye also yourselves [by an act of faith] to be dead indeed unto sin, but alive unto God through Jesus Christ our Lord" (v. 11). We are to count this true in our lives.

All four of the Gospel writers had something to say on this subject. In Matthew 10:38,39 we read: "And he that taketh not his cross [death], and followeth after me, is not worthy of me. He that findeth his life shall lose it [trying to find his own way in this earthly life]: and he that loseth his life for my sake shall find it." If we are willing to give up our self-life for His sake, we really begin to live.

In Mark 8:34,38 we learn: "And when he had called the people unto him with his disciples also, he said unto them, Whosoever will come after me, let him deny himself, and take up his cross, and follow me. . . . Whosoever therefore shall be ashamed of me and of my words in this adulterous and sinful generation; of him also shall the Son of man be ashamed, when he cometh in the glory of his Father with the holy angels."

Paul provides a practical demonstration of this. When told by friends that if he went to Jerusalem he would be made a prisoner and possibly put to death, he said, "But none of these things move me, neither count I my life dear unto myself, so that I might finish my course with joy, and the ministry, which I have received of the Lord Jesus, to testify the gospel of the grace of God" (Acts 20:24). He was willing to lay down his life if it would mean completing the ministry that God had entrusted him with. His self-life had no value to him. This was Elisha's attitude also when he followed Elijah to the Jordan and beyond.

A very important decision must be made by all of us. Our Lord said in Luke 14:26,27, "If any man come to me, and hate not his father, and mother, and wife, and children, and breth-ren, and sisters, yea, and his own life also, he cannot be my disciple. And whosoever doth not bear his cross, and come after me, cannot be my disciple." We may be children of God, but we cannot be disciples in the sense of one who is learning and serving unless we put God in first place—ahead of all earthly ties or ambitions.

In John's Gospel our Lord said, "I say unto you, Except a corn of wheat fall into the ground and die, it abideth alone: but if it die, it bringeth forth much fruit" (12:24).

Along this same line, and encouraging us to make a decision, are our Lord's words in Luke 14:33: "So likewise, whosoever he be of you that forsaketh not all that he hath, he cannot be my disciple." This is why Paul said in Philippians 3 that he counted all his personal and early religious accomplishments as loss for Christ: "I count all things but loss for the excellency of the knowledge of Christ Jesus my Lord" (v. 8). Is Christ our Lord? If so, we will not hesitate to go on with Him.

Turning back again to the story of Elijah and Elisha, we learn in II Kings 2:7,8: "And fifty men of the sons of the prophets went, and stood to view afar off: and they two [Elijah and Elisha] stood by Jordan. And Elijah took his mantle, and wrapped it together, and smote the waters, and they were divided hither and thither, so that they two went over on dry ground." This was an act of faith on Elijah's part. God held back the waters of the Jordan River because of this expression of faith, and His two servants committed themselves to Him. They did not ask how God held back the waters but trusted Him to do it.

Death to the self-life requires faith. We accept by faith our death in Christ. We do not understand this necessarily, but we accept it by faith, and we find that it works. When we believe God in these matters, He takes over. The Christian life is a life of faith, and every step is a step of faith. "Faith cometh by hearing, and hearing by the word of God" (Rom. 10:17). Thus the life of faith is the life of obedience to God's revealed Word.

The Principle of Faith

Elijah did not stand on the banks of the river waiting for God to do something. True faith results in action. The river had

159

to part, and Elijah struck it with his mantle. God had parted the river for Joshua and the Israelites long before this; so this particular miracle was not new. What God did once, surely He would do again. The waters parted as Elijah desired.

Faith was in operation as he and Elisha walked through the bed of the river. The water suddenly stopped as though someone had built a dam. No dam was visible just as the hand of God is not visible. Water that had already passed continued to recede, and soon the two men were able to cross on dry ground.

While they were passing through the bed of the river, they very possibly saw the water being piled up as the river continued to flow downstream. How could they be sure that this body of water would not suddenly give way and drown them? This was where faith entered in again. Elijah not only had faith in the parting of the water, but both prophets demonstrated faith by passing through the bed of the river. This shows that we must by faith appropriate what God has done for us. We must accept it as a fact and venture out on the basis of it. It is not merely a matter of saying, "Lord, I believe that You can deliver me from sin and its enslavement." Faith without works is a dead faith. We must act on it as did these two men in crossing the Jordan.

Each of the steps in which Elisha journeyed with Elijah was a matter of faith. It raises this question: "How do I know that I am separated to God? Does the reality of my separation depend on how earnest I was at the time I surrendered my life?" Not necessarily. Earnestness has its place, but the essential ingredient was faith when we said yes to God. We place ourselves in His hands, and He does the separating. This sanctification, or separation, is God's doing. He separates us to Himself.

Then what about entering into spiritual warfare? How do I know that God will answer my prayer and accept my decision? God will do this because He has said so. We step out in faith, and this applies to every aspect of our Christian life. Only as God sees us moving forward will He be able to work on our behalf. We must move forward by faith with Him.

This is a lesson the Lord taught my wife and me personally many years ago. The very incident of the Israelites crossing the Jordan River was the Scripture passage the Lord used to emphasize to us that He wanted us to step out by faith. This was more than 40 years ago when God brought us to Lincoln, Nebraska, to begin the Back to the Bible Broadcast. We had to step out in faith, burning all bridges behind us. We trusted only in God, for there was no visible means of support from any other source.

It has been the same principle of faith that we have sought to follow all through the years since then. We sign contracts with stations, not waiting until the money is available. When we believe God wants us to go ahead, we do so. We undertake missionary work by faith, and God has met the needs.

Elisha's Request

After Elijah and Elisha had crossed the river, Elijah said to the younger man, "Ask what I shall do for thee, before I be taken away from thee. And Elisha said, I pray thee, let a double portion of thy spirit be upon me" (II Kings 2:9).

Elijah's question had unlimited potential. Elisha was first to ask what he wanted Elijah to do for him. This threw the gate wide open, so to speak, to this young man. This clearly shows us what God will do for us, for Elijah could do for Elisha only what God would give. Our Saviour said in Luke 11:13, "If ye then, being evil, know how to give good gifts unto your children: how much more shall your heavenly Father give the Holy Spirit to them that ask him?" How many individuals responded to this promise before Pentecost? Another great promise is found in Matthew 7:7,8: "Ask, and it shall be given you; seek, and ye shall find; knock, and it shall be opened unto you: for everyone that asketh receiveth; and he that seeketh findeth; and to him that knocketh it shall be opened." If we do not receive from God, it is because we have not asked, according to James 4:2.

Let us not blame God if we do not see in our lives what we think ought to be there. We have either not surrendered our lives to the Lord, or we have not accepted by faith what God has already accomplished for us in Christ Jesus, or we simply have not asked.

On this particular occasion, Elisha showed what was deep in his own heart. His answer is something for us to ponder as we think of what the goal in our life might be. Is it success of some kind? Is it something that God can honor?

The various testings Elisha had passed through from Gilgal to the time when he was asked what Elijah could do for him were stepping-stones of faith. They led up to that great climax. Elisha's answer was "I pray thee, let a double portion of thy spirit be upon me" (II Kings 2:9).

This was in the spirit of Paul's aspiration when he declared that he had left all things behind him in order that he might attain to the excellency of the knowledge of Christ Jesus (see Phil. 3:8). He wanted to know Christ and the "power of his resurrection, and the fellowship of his sufferings, being made conformable unto his death" that he might experience daily the resurrection life of Christ in him (v. 10). He did not feel that he had already attained this, but he followed Christ and pressed "toward the mark for the prize of the high calling of God in Christ Jesus" (v. 14).

The question put to Elisha cannot be put to just anybody, for not all are ready for it. But this verse in the Psalms is the key to receiving from God the best things: "Delight thyself also in the Lord; and he shall give thee the desires of thine heart" (37:4).

I have meditated on this verse for many, many years, and though I have experienced it in part, I am still conscious of failure to always delight myself in the Lord.

When our goal in life is to do the will of God, He will show us what we should make our purpose in life.

Paul's prayer for the Ephesians and for us is: "That the God of our Lord Jesus Christ, the Father of glory, may give unto you the spirit of wisdom and revelation in the knowledge of him: the eyes of your understanding being enlightened; that ye may know what is the hope of his calling, and what the riches of the glory of his inheritance in the saints" (Eph. 1:17,18).

There was an unlimited potential before Elisha, and he wasted no time in making known his God-given desire.

Elisha Given Elijah's Mantle

Elisha had sat at the feet of Elijah for about ten years. He had seen what it meant to be a servant of God, to have a surrendered heart and a holy life. He also witnessed how God honors such a person. For his own part, Elisha was totally consecrated to the Lord. He had passed many tests from the day that Elijah had cast his mantle on him, and in the events leading up to the crossing of the Jordan, he had again proved that he wanted to obey the Lord completely.

The casting of the mantle upon him was significant. In Jewish customs it was the sign of adoption as a son. In Elisha's case it meant that he was adopted by Elijah to be a spiritual heir of the prophet. Just as the firstborn in Israel had the right to a double portion of the inheritance, so Elisha, in asking for a double portion of the spirit that rested upon Elijah, was being consistent with the position he held. He was not necessarily the first individual Elijah had led into a true worship of the Lord, but he was picked to be the spiritual son and successor of this prophet of God.

Elisha did not ask for more of the Holy Spirit. A person either receives the Holy Spirit or does not. A true believer always receives Him. The question we need to ask is "How much does the Holy Spirit have of me?"

In asking for a double portion of Elijah's spirit, Elisha was referring to the ministry he was to inherit. It is no accident that twice as many miracles were performed by Elisha than by Elijah, and he ministered twice as long as Elijah. This was not something that was done without absolute surrender on his part to the Spirit of God. Such a ministry cannot be fulfilled on the human level. It is a divine work in the first place and must be energized by God.

Elijah's answer is given in II Kings 2:10: "And he said, Thou hast asked a hard thing: nevertheless, if thou see me when I am taken from thee, it shall be so unto thee; but if not, it shall not be so." This was not something Elijah himself could promise, for it was not his prerogative to give. With his prophetic insight, however, he could say to Elisha, "If I am carried away in full view of you, then your request is granted; if not, it is refused." If Elisha saw Elijah being translated, then he should accept it as a sign from God that his request had been granted.

Only a man whose spiritual qualities were right before God would be permitted to view this actual scene. Just as there are sounds we cannot hear, there are realities we cannot see. The chariot of fire and the horses of fire were real, though not all who were watching Elijah and Elisha saw them. The Bible tells us that God has appointed angels as guardians of His people, and part of His care for us comes through them. Little children have guardian angels, according to the Scriptures (see Matt. 18:10), but no guardian angel is humanly visible.

Fifty young prophets stood by the river watching, but they did not see what Elisha saw. The Spirit of God did not give them the spiritual insight needed because they were not prepared for it. Elisha had passed the test of Bethel, which speaks of separation; the test of Jericho, which speaks of warfare; and the test of Jordan, which speaks of death and resurrection. These others had not.

In II Kings 6 is a very good illustration of this whole matter. Elisha was established as God's prophet and was, of course, the target for God's enemies. Ben-hadad, king of Syria, made war on Israel but found that the secret plans that he talked of in his private chambers were known almost immediately to the king of Israel. The Syrian king learned that Elisha the prophet was informing the Israelites of his plans, and so he determined to capture him.

Soon after, he sent an army to surround the city of Dothan with the hope of taking Elisha. The prophet's servant discovered this when he arose early one morning and found horses and chariots encircling the town. He ran to his master terrified.

Elisha said to him, "Fear not: for they that be with us are more than they that be with them" (v. 16). Then Elisha prayed a remarkable prayer: "Lord, I pray thee, open his eyes, that he may see. And the Lord opened the eyes of the young man; and he saw: and, behold, the mountain was full of horses and chariots of fire round about Elisha" (v. 17). It took a special manifestation of God's power for this young man to see the spiritual forces around the city of Dothan.

Paul's prayer for the Ephesians and for us is not that our physical eyes shall see things that ordinarily they cannot see but that our spiritual vision shall be clarified so our faith will claim God's promises. Paul prayed for "the spirit of wisdom and revelation in the knowledge of him: the eyes of your understanding being enlightened; that ye may know what is the hope of his calling, and what the riches of the glory of his inheritance in the saints" (Eph. 1:17,18).

Elisha did see Elijah's translation, for we learn: "And it came to pass, as they still went on, and talked, that, behold, there appeared a chariot of fire, and horses of fire, and parted them both asunder; and Elijah went up by a whirlwind into heaven" (II Kings 2:11).

His great request was answered!

Chapter 14

Elisha Accepts Elijah's Unfinished Task

The horses of fire and the chariots of fire, I believe, speak of Elijah's fiery message. He was a prophet of fire. And he came and went like a whirlwind. It surely is quite significant that this is the closing scene of Elijah's earthly ministry.

It was also, of course, the beginning of Elisha's own ministry as he fulfilled the responsibilities left by his former teacher. This is one reason why he cried, "My father, my father, the chariot of Israel, and the horsemen thereof. And he saw him no more: and he took hold of his own clothes, and rent them in two pieces" (II Kings 2:12). As Elisha recognized the seriousness of his responsibility, he realized that in himself he could not fulfill it. Elijah had been like a father to him. Now the older prophet was gone, and this left Elisha in the forefront of the battle.

I personally have some understanding of the situation. On December 22, 1945, I stood in a mortuary in Kansas, looking on the face of the man who had meant more to me than any other person on earth—my own father. Several friends and relatives were standing by when I found myself overcome by emotion and wept. Mother came over to me, patted me on the shoulder and said, "Now son, now son." I told her that it was not because Dad was gone that I was weeping, though I would miss his fellowship. It was the sudden realization that many responsibilities that had been on his shoulders were now transferred to mine. I could no longer go to him and ask him questions or pray with him or receive counsel from him. The realization of this overwhelming responsibility upset me emotionally.

Elijah, through his ministry and his prayer life, had been a protector of Israel. This is why Elisha cried, "The chariot of Israel, and the horsemen thereof" (v. 12). Moses did the same for the Israelites in his day as he interceded for them before God.

I believe the tearing of his garments indicated Elisha's recognition of his own inability and insufficiency. It spoke of his brokenness before God and his appeal to God for His divine strength.

I heard a sermon once by a dear brother who came to pastor a church that had been ministered to for more than one generation by a dearly loved man of God. This former pastor had been one of God's great, stalwart soldiers, a spiritual giant in many ways. For a new pastor to pick up where this former pastor had left off was a difficult assignment. Some in the church had known only one pastor in 40 years. He meant everything to them, and it was natural that they would judge a new preacher by the pattern set by the one who had gone to be with the Lord.

The sermon I heard by the new pastor was one of the finest on this subject I have ever heard. His text was from Joshua 1: "Moses my servant is dead" (v. 2). The man who had been Joshua's leader and Israel's leader for 40 years was gone. This, however, was not all that God had to say. He continued, "Now therefore arise, go over this Jordan, thou, and all this people, unto the land which I do give to them, even to the children of Israel. Every place that the sole of your foot shall tread upon, that have I given unto you, as I said unto Moses. From the wilderness and this Lebanon even unto the great river, the river Euphrates, all the land of the Hittites, and unto the great sea toward the going down of the sun, shall be your coast. There shall not any man be able to stand before thee all the days of thy life: as I was with Moses, so I will be with thee: I will not fail thee, nor forsake thee. Be strong and of a good courage" (vv. 2-6).

This pastor went on to say, "I realize that many of you wonder if I can fill the shoes of your former pastor. I can never do that. I did not come here to fill his shoes. I would have had to turn down this invitation to pastor this flock if it were not for the consolation that I have from this message from God to Joshua when he said, 'As I was with Moses, so I will be with thee.' "

Elijah was gone, but God was still present. God is the everliving One, and though His servants are removed from this earthly scene, He continues, for He never fails. This was what gave Elisha the courage to accept the challenge, even though he did it with a broken heart. His acceptance is demonstrated through his picking up the mantle of Elijah. "He took up also the mantle of Elijah that fell from him, and went back, and stood by the bank of Jordan" (II Kings 2:13). This garment was a loose cloak thrown around the shoulders and had become the recognized dress of the prophets of Jehovah. Elisha entered into that office accepting the gift of prophecy by faith.

Picking up Elijah's mantle meant that Elisha would stand with God just as the older prophet had done. He was assured he could do it because he had seen Elijah's translation and because the prophet's garment had been left behind for him.

Recrossing the Jordan

Elisha returned to the Jordan and "took the mantle of Elijah that fell from him, and smote the waters, and said, Where is the Lord God of Elijah? and when he also had smitten the waters, they parted hither and thither: and Elisha went over" (II Kings 2:14). The Lord made it possible for Elisha to cross the Jordan on dry ground as He had done for Elijah. He was gone, but his God remained.

It is very possible that Elisha did not feel any different when he found himself endued with power from above. There is no record that he had a great emotional experience; nevertheless, he had come to a place where an act of faith was needed, and he acted. There was no doubting of God in this action of Elisha's. Rather it was an act of confidence because he believed that God, who had given Elijah power, was now empowering him.

About 3000 years have gone by since those days. Has God died? Has He lost power? Is the lack of faith so evident among many people today due to God's failure or our own spiritual deterioration? This is an age when we are inclined to be dazzled by the inventions of men, but God is the same God now as He was in Elijah and Elisha's time. His power has not diminished. The question is "Have we made this God our God?" Someone once said, "Men are looking for better methods, and God is looking for better men." Elijah and Elisha were specially appointed by God to do His work.

There was still another reason why God demonstrated His power for Elisha in parting the waters of the Jordan. The sons of the prophets had watched what they could see of the parting of these two men. At least Elijah's mantle would be visible to them. They saw Elisha pick it up and then smite the waters of the Jordan so that they parted. We read: "When the sons of the prophets which were to view at Jericho saw him, they said, The spirit of Elijah doth rest on Elisha. And they came to meet him, and bowed themselves to the ground before him" (v. 15). There was a revival among them when they saw the power of God upon the new leader.

God is still able to bring revival today, and He will when He finds hearts responding to Him and submitting themselves completely to His leading and direction. Revival is not necessarily brought about by prayer. It is accomplished when we believe God and trust Him.

Elisha's Fourfold Heritage From Elijah

There is no use in studying the Bible if we do not apply its truths to our lives. This is what we mean by meditating on the Word. We look into the Word of God, which serves as a mirror and reveals our sin; then we turn to God and ask Him to cleanse us and to change us to His glory. The psalmist said, "Thy word have I hid in mine heart, that I might not sin against thee" (Ps. 119:11). Bible truth will mean nothing to us unless we apply it to our lives.

Elijah's Mantle

The first part of the heritage Elisha received was the mantle of his master. When Elijah cast it off, he threw off forever the burden of his earthly ministry and commission. It is true that, according to some interpretations of prophecy, he will again appear on the earthly scene, but that task will not have anything to do with his ministry of some 3000 years ago. The commission laid down by Elijah was part of the heritage he decreed to Elisha so the work begun by the older prophet would be carried on to its consummation.

This was symbolically presented in the mantle that Elijah dropped. The younger man accepted it, but it would have been of little significance had not God's power been given along with it. God's work, though it is done by people, must be done in His wisdom and strength.

There is an important lesson in this for us. Suppose Elisha had said, "No, I won't have anything to do with this mantle," meaning that he would not have anything to do with carrying on the work that Elijah had left. This would have been a serious breakdown in the relaying of God's work from one servant to another. The Lord Jesus said in John 15:16, "Ye have not chosen me, but I have chosen you, and ordained you, that ye should go and bring forth fruit, and that your fruit should remain." Here we have the evidence that we are divinely commissioned to carry on the message begun by our Lord.

In Acts 1 we have the record of our Saviour's last meeting with His disciples before His ascension: "And, being assembled together with them, commanded them that they should not depart from Jerusalem, but wait for the promise of the Father, which, saith he, ye have heard of me. For John truly baptized with water; but ye shall be baptized with the Holy Ghost not many days hence" (vv. 4,5). The disciples were not to leave Jerusalem until they had witnessed the coming of the Holy Spirit. They were concerned about the coming of the kingdom, but the Lord reminded them that the kingdom was not a subject they needed to be concerned about at that time.

Their great need was to wait as He had commanded, for He said, "Ye shall receive power, after that the Holy Ghost is come upon you: and ye shall be witnesses unto me both in Jerusalem, and in all Judaea, and in Samaria, and unto the uttermost part of the earth. And when he had spoken these things, while they beheld, he was taken up; and a cloud received him out of their sight" (vv. 8,9). The same truth is approached from another angle by the Apostle Paul in II Corinthians 5:18: "And all things are of God, who hath reconciled us to himself by Jesus Christ, and hath given to us the ministry of reconciliation." In the next two verses he told us what message we are to give to others: "To wit, that God was in Christ, reconciling the world unto himself, not imputing their trespasses unto them; and hath committed unto us the word of reconciliation. Now then we are ambassadors for Christ, as though God did beseech you by us: we pray you in Christ's stead, be ye reconciled to God" (vv. 19,20).

We, then, like Elisha, have been commissioned to finish a task begun by another. We have been chosen of God for this purpose as was Elisha. But just as he could not do the work in his own power—and God did not expect him to—neither can we carry on in our own strength.

God calls us to absolute surrender of ourselves so that His work through us will be done as He planned it. We are to glorify God in our body and in our spirit, which are God's (I Cor. 6:20).

We will be called upon at the Judgment Seat of Christ to answer for what we have done with the heritage received from our Lord. This was of great concern to Paul, for he said, "Wherefore we labour, that, whether present or absent, we may be accepted of [pleasing to] him. For we must all appear before the judgment seat of Christ; that everyone may receive the things done in his body, according to that he hath done, whether it be good or bad" (II Cor. 5:9,10). Elisha received a call from heaven to go and do God's work. We, too, have received such a call to complete the work our Saviour began.

Elijah's God

The second part of the heritage was that Elijah's God remained with Elisha. Not only did the mantle speak of the call to the work, but he also had the assurance that the God who worked miracles through Elijah was with him. This is why he said as he smote the waters of the Jordan: "Where is the Lord God of Elijah?" (II Kings 2:14). The mantle would have been useless if the God of Elijah had not proven Himself to be on the side of Elisha.

We not only have been called to work for the Lord, but we also have the assurance of His presence with us. Not only did our Lord say, "Go ye into all the world, and preach the gospel" (Mark 16:15), but He also said, "And, lo, I am with you alway" (Matt. 28:20). We direct our prayers to the Father through the Son. We can ask, "Where is the God and the Father of our Lord Jesus Christ?" in the same sense Elisha asked, "Where is the Lord God of Elijah?"

The presence of God with us is deeper and fuller than we often think, for the Lord's prayer in John 17 is for our oneness with Him and the Father. "That they all may be one; as thou, Father, art in me, and I in thee, that they also may be one in us: that the world may believe that thou hast sent me" (v. 21). In verse 23 of the same chapter of John, our Saviour said, "I in them, and thou in me, that they may be made perfect in one; and that the world may know that thou hast sent me, and hast loved them, as thou hast loved me."

Previous to this time our Lord had said, "If a man love me, he will keep my words: and my Father will love him, and we will come unto him, and make our abode with him" (14:23). There should be no question, then, about the fact that God is with us. He not only has sent us out to be His ambassadors, but we have the firm assurance of His indwelling presence.

Elijah's Spirit

When the waters parted for Elisha at the Jordan River, there was the witness that the Spirit of God was upon him

(II Kings 2:14). The same Spirit that energized Elijah energized Elisha. Without the power and the presence of the Holy Spirit, Elisha's ministry would have been impossible.

Elisha may not have felt a bit different when he inherited the Spirit's presence and fullness in his life, but he accepted it as a fact by faith. This is something we must do also.

In writing to the Ephesians, Paul said, "In whom ye also trusted, after that ye heard the word of truth, the gospel of your salvation: in whom also after that ye believed [upon believing], ye were sealed with that holy Spirit of promise, which is the earnest of our inheritance until the redemption of the purchased possession, unto the praise of his glory" (Eph. 1:13,14). We still have the complete inheritance coming, but the down payment, which is the Holy Spirit, has already been made.

It is no wonder, then, that in Ephesians 5 we are told not to be drunk with wine but to be filled with the Holy Spirit (v. 18).

The sons of the prophets witnessed the power of God on Elisha, and they testified that the Spirit who energized Elijah rested on their new leader.

The Spirit of God is also given to us to fulfill the appointed task entrusted to us. There is no excuse, then, for us to say that we cannot do what God wants us to do. God does not ask us to do it but wants us to let the Holy Spirit do it in and through us. When we present ourselves completely to Him, then He can accomplish His purposes in our lives.

Elijah's Office

Elisha was also the heir of the prophetic office. By this, we mean that he was to carry on the work that Elijah had begun. Elijah was a prophet, and he had been God's man to rebuke the nation for its Baal worship. Elisha was to continue this ministry.

It is part of our heritage to carry on the work that our Saviour began. He had a physical body in which He was born, lived, died and was buried. His body was resurrected and glorified, and in that body He is coming to earth again. But he has another Body — the mystical Body, or Church, of which you and I are members. He has left us here on the earth

173

to carry on the work. The Book of the Acts opens with the words, "The former treatise have I made, O Theophilus, of all that Jesus began both to do and teach, until the day in which he was taken up, after that he through the Holy Ghost had given commandments unto the apostles whom he had chosen" (1:1,2). He made very clear to the disciples what their worldwide responsibility was.

How part of this was carried on is revealed in Acts 13, where we learn that, as the early church ministered to the Lord, the Holy Spirit said, "Separate me Barnabas and Saul for the work whereunto I have called them" (Acts 13:2). According to Paul in II Corinthians 5:20, we are to carry on the great ministry in the place of our Lord Jesus Himself.

Perhaps no clearer words concerning this can be found anywhere than in John 20:21-23: "Then said Jesus to them again, Peace be unto you: as my Father hath sent me, even so send I you. And when he had said this, he breathed on them, and saith unto them, Receive ye the Holy Ghost: whose soever sins ye remit, they are remitted unto them; and whose soever sins ye retain, they are retained." This is a glorious heritage the Lord has left us! Let us accept it and act upon it.

Chapter 15

Looking Back and Looking Ahead

The reason for reemphasizing some of the following aspects of Elijah's life is that we might not overlook any basic key to the understanding of the significance of his life to us.

A Man of Like Nature

First, the Bible says Elijah was a man subject to like passions, or as another translation says it, "a man of like nature" (James 5:17, RSV). God permits us to see where Elijah failed so that we need not think we are dealing with a perfect man. He was human just as we are; what sets him apart from most of us is that he fully believed God.

What Elijah accomplished is possible to us today if God should call us to such a ministry and if we will believe and trust Him for it. It is true that we know nothing of Elijah's family background or of his life before his public ministry began. He appeared suddenly, and he went away suddenly. Yet he was a man who had the same fallen nature that we have; he was subject to temptations similar to ours; he faced the same tests and trials that all humans face. He walked with the same God we have the privilege of walking with. He sought the Lord for the same things that you and I seek Him for. We may seek the Lord as Elijah did, for our Saviour made God's will very plain: "Ask, and it shall be given you; seek, and ye shall find; knock, and it shall be opened unto you" (Matt. 7:7). The Apostle Paul said, "I can do all things through Christ which strengtheneth me" (Phil. 4:13).

Paul was no different than we are, but he was called for a special task. He, too, like Elijah, gave himself wholeheartedly to the Lord to be used. God does not call us to be a Paul or an Elijah or an Elisha, but He calls on us to trust Him as they did and to be as fully committed to His will as they were. He has a task for us to do, and He equips us with all the necessary talents and abilities to do it. If we will present our bodies to Him, He will work in us and through us. Remember, the Scriptures say, "It is God which worketh in you both to will and to do of his good pleasure" (2:13).

A Man of Faith

Second, Elijah walked by faith and not by sight. This makes all the difference in the world in the effectiveness of a life committed to the Lord. Because he was a man of faith, he could live by the Brook Cherith even while it was drying up. The ravens brought him food in the morning and in the evening just as God said they would, and apparently it did not bother Elijah one bit that the water was slowly disappearing. By an act of faith he went to live there in the first place, and he trusted God throughout that experience. God told him what to do, and that settled it for Elijah (I Kings 17:2-7).

Later he went to live in the home of a widow who expected to cook her last morsel of bread, and then she and her son would await death by starvation. But God multiplied the meal in the barrel and the oil in the cruse, and all three lived on that food for several years. God provided day by day as the need arose. He did not give them large stores that would last for years, but His promise was that the daily supply would not cease, and it never did (vv. 8-16).

Are we learning to trust God daily? He never forgets or sleeps. He is always taking care of His own and is constantly looking for a child of His who will dare to believe Him. Elijah dared to consider God faithful. How often we have made God a liar by not believing Him! Nothing honors Him more than faith, but nothing so dishonors Him as unbelief.

When Elijah heard God's word, he believed it and acted on it. "Faith cometh by hearing, and hearing by the word of God" (Rom. 10:17). Perhaps our faith is not larger than it is because we have not studied the Word. Our faith will not grow if we do not spend time in the Word of God itself.

I have talked to many people with spiritual problems, and when I have asked them about their personal devotional life, I often found it very meager. They may read a little before they go to bed at night, but they do not read the Bible in the morning because they are so busy. Ignoring the Word is a basic reason for our problems.

It may not always be easy to take time in the morning for personal devotions, but if we want to grow spiritually, we must take that time. We must get our sense of values properly adjusted and realize what is most important for our lives. What do we consider more important — what we are doing or what God wants to do in our lives? Starting the day with God is the most important thing for any of us. Elijah heard God's word and believed it and acted upon it.

Faith without works is dead (see James 2:17), but Elijah's faith wasn't dead. He acted on what he believed. Obedience is simply faith in action. Obedience trusts God and goes ahead.

A Man of Separation

Third, Elijah walked in complete separation from the evil around him. In many places people want Christian workers who are good mixers. They say this is necessary if we are going to win young people or some other group that is hard to reach. We feel they cannot be raised to our spiritual standard; so we get down to their low spiritual level. This is not the way God wants to reach them, and it is not the way Elijah lived.

We are not called to win the world to Christ but to witness against its sin using the Word of God. This is to be done by our life as well as by the Word. Elijah separated himself from the evil around him. He was a pilgrim and a stranger who never fraternized with evil in order to win evil men to the Lord.

He lived among such people, but he was not one with them in practice and belief. No doubt, many considered him unsocial and as having a "holier than thou" attitude. If we are right with God, what difference will it make how we are charged by those who disagree with us? Let them go ahead and say what they want to say if our own lives before God are right and our hearts are humble. If we do manifest a "holier than thou" attitude, then we are at fault. But just because someone accuses us of having such an attitude does not mean it is true.

A biblical principle is laid down for us in Hebrews 13:13,14: "Let us go forth therefore unto him without the camp, bearing his reproach. For here have we no continuing city, but we seek one to come." Though this was not written in Elijah's day, nevertheless, this was the principle by which he lived. He was willing to suffer what was necessary in order to live for God. He followed God and God alone.

This does not mean that we have to shut ourselves off from all contact and all responsibility to the society in which we live. We have to weigh our different responsibilities in the light of God's call to us for service. We need civic-minded Christians, but they must by all means maintain a separated, holy life.

I am constantly invited to join this group or that group, but I realize if I were to do so, I would have to neglect the work to which God has called me. To let lesser things interfere would be to disobey God.

A Man of Intercession

Fourth, Elijah was mighty in his intercession. This was not an easy task but a hard one. His heart was constantly burdened for the people of Israel. His prayer on Mount Carmel is typical of the burden of his heart: "Lord God of Abraham, Isaac, and of Israel, let it be known this day that thou art God in Israel, and that I am thy servant, and that I have done all these things at thy word. Hear me, O Lord, hear me, that this people may know that thou art the Lord God, and that thou hast turned their heart back again" (I Kings 18:36,37). Elijah was a great intercessor for his people. His prayers were largely on their behalf. This was one reason why God gave him such glorious vindication time after time.

A Man of Courage

Fifth, Elijah was a man of great courage. In order to understand this better, we must distinguish clearly between natural bravery and spiritual boldness.

Elijah, when left to himself, was anything but brave. After he had dared to stand against Ahab and a hostile nation and the vindictive prophets of Baal, he fled when threatened by a woman (I Kings 18:21 — 19:3). As long as he dared to trust God he was as bold as a lion. The moment he took his eyes off God he was the opposite. The person who truly fears God does not fear other people.

God recorded all of this, not to excuse our sin but as a warning that when we do not stand with God, even for a moment, we will fail and fall. Though greatly honored by God, Elijah's sins were not glossed over. Though he was endued with the power of the Holy Spirit in order to accomplish the tasks assigned to him, sin was never eradicated from his life. In his own flesh he was still a sinful man. This is why we are warned that we should take heed, because the person who thinks he stands can easily fall (I Cor. 10:12).

We are just as dependent on God for the maintenance of our spiritual life and the spiritual graces He has given us as we are for God's bestowment of them on us in the first place.

God vindicated the ministry of Elijah by taking him home without dying. Human nature being what it is, he was probably branded an enthusiast, an alarmist, a firebrand, and his message was probably brushed aside. If he had died a natural death, some of these skeptics might have been confirmed in their unbelief. But when God took him away as He did, without dying, He placed His stamp of approval on the ministry of His prophet.

This is exactly what the Rapture will mean to unbelievers who presently poke fun at those who believe the Bible. This event will be one of the most nerve-shaking events in all history, when millions of these "fanatical, Bible-believing Christians" will suddenly be gone and the apostate, ecumenical church left. That great event will vindicate those who have dared to believe the old-fashioned truth of the Word of God.

A Man of Obedience

A sixth lesson we learn from Elijah's life is that it is not good for us to try to tell God how our lives should be lived. Elijah asked at one time that he might die, but God did not answer this plea, for He had something far better for His servant. God always has a better plan for us than we can ever devise; so let us never try to tell God what our lives should consist of.

Another thing we learn from Elijah's experience is that, though he did not pass through death, his translation helps us see what death is for the believer. It is not a state of being but an act. It is not a condition but a passage. There is no interval of unconsciousness. Death for the believer is being absent from the body and present with the Lord. By an act of birth we enter into natural life; by an act, called death, believers enter into real life.

The translation of the believer who will be on the earth when Christ returns for His Church is expressed very clearly in I Corinthians 15:51-53: "Behold, I shew you a mystery; We shall not all sleep, but we shall all be changed, in a moment, in the twinkling of an eye, at the last trump: for the trumpet shall sound, and the dead shall be raised incorruptible, and we shall be changed. For this corruptible must put on incorruption, and this mortal must put on immortality." This must be something like the experience of Elijah when he was translated.

Elijah's Rewards

Some of Elijah's rewards are presented in Scripture. Others, we are sure, will not be evident until we get to heaven.

This makes us consider some preliminary matters with regard to God's plans and the timing He ordains concerning those plans. We are admonished in Galatians 6:9: "Let us not be weary in well doing: for in due season we shall reap, if we faint not." God's plan for any of us contains a great deal of mystery, but we must trust Him. He has not told us to understand what He does but to trust what He does. He has a long-range plan for this world in which each one of us has a part if we walk in obedience to the Lord.

James threw further light on this subject: "Be patient therefore, brethren, unto the coming of the Lord. Behold, the husbandman waiteth for the precious fruit of the earth, and hath long patience for it, until he receive the early and latter rain. Be ye also patient; stablish your hearts: for the coming of the Lord draweth nigh. Grudge not one against another, brethren, lest ye be condemned: behold, the judge standeth before the door" (James 5:7-9). This again reminds us that we need patience with regard to the plans of God and constant trust in His wisdom, grace and power.

A third passage of Scripture that is very important is the last part of Hebrews 11. This particular chapter lists great men and women of faith and concludes with this final word concerning them: "(Of whom the world was not worthy:) they wandered in deserts, and in mountains, and in dens and caves of the earth. And these all, having obtained a good report through faith, received not the promise: God having provided some better thing for us, that they without us should not be made perfect" (vv. 38-40). *The Amplified Bible* translates this section as follows: "[Men] of whom the world was not worthy, roaming over the desolate places and the mountains, and [living] in caves and caverns and holes of the earth. And all of these, though they won divine approval by [means of] their faith, did not receive the fulfillment of what was promised, because God had us in mind and had something better and greater in view for us, so that they [these heroes and heroines of faith] should not come to perfection apart from us, [that is, before we could join them]."

Your Part and Mine Are Vital

God has one great long-range plan and program for man that began with Adam and will conclude with the renovation of the heavens and the earth. Every part of this program will fit together, and each believer will fill a place in it. We cannot see what is ahead, nor do we know all that has been accomplished in the past. We do not even know what all is being done for the Lord in our own generation. But each one of us, as we walk with the Lord, fits into the plan that ties in with what has gone on in past generations and prepares the way for what is coming in future generations. That is why it is so essential for us to be obedient in every detail of our Christian experience. We may think our part is small and wonder how God could use us in His overall plan, but God overlooks nothing, and to Him nothing is unimportant. We must be sure that we fulfill the requirements He lays down for us.

An illustration will help us here. In the plan of God Moses was God's great lawgiver. That was one of the great contributions he made during his service. Elijah, on the other hand, was God's great reformer to bring God's people back to the Law of Moses. Each servant of the Lord, then, contributes his part to God's work, and all will be included in the rewards given. Hebrews 11 provides us with a small list of some who have had a part in God's work. This list is increased generation after generation, and you and I have a share in it.

Elijah on the Mount of Transfiguration

Elijah was not only chosen to witness in the days of Ahab but also on two occasions following that, hundreds of years apart. His earthly ministry possibly lasted for only 15 years, but he ministered again briefly on the Mount of Transfiguration and will come back to earth to witness at a time still future.

When Elijah went to Horeb and heard the still, small voice of God, he probably had little understanding of what God wanted from him. He had been discouraged because the revival he was looking for did not take place in his generation. It is very likely that when he appeared with the Lord Jesus on the Mount of Transfiguration, he understood in a better way what God's program involved.

This was a very important event in the life of our Lord and is recorded for us by three of the Gospel writers, Matthew in chapter 17, Mark in chapter 9 and Luke in chapter 9. Our Lord went to the top of a mountain to pray and took with him Peter, James and John. While He prayed, "the fashion of his countenance was altered, and his raiment was white and glistering. And, behold, there talked with him two men, which were Moses and Elias [Elijah]" (Luke 9:29,30).

This remarkable experience took place soon after the Lord had asked the disciples how people were identifying Him. Some thought He was John the Baptist, some thought He was Elijah, still others thought He was one of the other prophets.

Then Peter spoke up and said, "Thou art the Christ, the Son of the living God" (Matt. 16:16). Following this event, Jesus told His disciples about His death on the cross and His resurrection from the grave. Peter, not understanding the meaning of Christ's words and what God's program involved, rebuked Him: "Be it far from thee, Lord: this shall not be unto thee" (v. 22).

This was one reason why Moses and Elijah were included in the Transfiguration experience. They had played a significant part in Israel's history—Moses as the giver of the Law and Elijah as the prophet who warned his people of the judgment that followed the breaking of the Law. Now they had come to meet the Saviour and talk with Him concerning a matter of even greater importance. They spoke to Him of His "decease which he should accomplish at Jerusalem" (Luke 9:31). The word "decease" is literally "exodus." They not only talked about His death, but they probably also talked about every part of the program of God that was ahead. Christ's death on Calvary was very near, and Moses and Elijah now could see what it all meant. Moses could now understand how the Law was given to bring people to Christ. Elijah now understood why he had preached judgment in his day but did not see the completion of that program. Now he was about to see the grace of God manifested on behalf of all mankind. The suffering and death of Jesus were the heart of it.

The Lord was to die and to be buried, but that was not all. They spoke of His "exodus," and that would include His rising from the grave and His departure to heaven.

These men spoke to our Saviour about His death and resurrection in the hearing of the disciples, and this gave them a better understanding of God's program also. It was possibly also an encouragement for the Lord, who was both God and man. He was facing death as a man, which made this a serious hour for Him. So Moses and Elijah spoke to Him concerning the coming events. Elijah in particular, knowing something of the meaning of the still, small voice, would talk about the grace of God that was to be manifested.

Elijah's Final Witnessing

The Bible tells us that Elijah will take part in one further act on the earth. The prophecy concerning this is in Malachi 4:5,6: "Behold, I will send you Elijah the prophet before the coming of the great and dreadful day of the Lord: and he shall turn the heart of the fathers to the children, and the heart of the children to their fathers, lest I come and smite the earth with a curse." This was foreshadowed in the coming of John the Baptist, but John made it very clear that he was not Elijah.

In Zechariah we learn that two olive trees will witness in a special way for the Lord in the latter days (4:2,3). Further details are given in the Book of the Revelation: "And I will give power unto my two witnesses, and they shall prophesy a thousand two hundred and threescore days, clothed in sackcloth. These are the two olive trees, and the two candlesticks standing before the God of the earth. And if any man will hurt them, fire proceedeth out of their mouth, and devoureth their enemies: and if any man will hurt them, he must in this manner be killed" (11:3-5). This is the very kind of thing that we saw in the experience of Elijah. Soldiers were sent to take him, but he prayed down fire from God, which devoured them.

The passage in Revelation deals with the second half of the seven-year Tribulation. These witnesses will have the power to shut up heaven so that it does not rain, and they will have the power to turn the waters to blood and to smite the earth with plagues as often as they will (see v. 6). The withholding of the rain reminds us of Elijah, and turning the water into blood and smiting the earth with plagues was done previously through Moses.

Though Moses is not spoken of in the Bible as coming back again in the sense that Elijah is spoken of, it seems reasonable to suppose that he is the second witness. He was on the Mount of Transfiguration with Elijah and the Saviour. We would not be dogmatic about this, for others identify the second witness as Enoch because, as they point out, he did not die. But we know that one of them is Elijah. We further read concerning them: "And when they shall have finished their testimony, the beast that ascendeth out of the bottomless pit shall make war against them, and shall overcome them, and kill them. And their dead bodies shall lie in the street of the great city, which spiritually is called Sodom and Egypt, where also our Lord was crucified [old Jerusalem]. And they of the people and kindreds and tongues and nations shall see their dead bodies three days and an half, and shall not suffer their dead bodies to be put in graves. And they that dwell upon the earth shall rejoice over them, and make merry, and shall send gifts one to another; because these two prophets tormented them that dwelt on the earth. And after three days and an half the spirit of life from God entered into them, and they stood upon their feet; and great fear fell upon them which saw them. And they heard a great voice from heaven saying unto them, Come up hither. And they ascended up to heaven in a cloud; and their enemies beheld them" (vv. 7-12). This is undoubtedly the reward that God will give Elijah for his faithfulness.

We, too, shall be rewarded if we are faithful and true witnesses. If we are not ashamed of Him and suffer with Him, we shall rule and reign with Him.

Chapter 16

Elijah's God Still Lives

Assured of the fact that a double portion of Elijah's spirit rested on him and knowing that the prophetic office was now his to carry on, Elisha demonstrated his faith when he came to the Jordan River and struck it with the mantle. He asked this great question: "Where is the Lord God of Elijah?" (II Kings 2:14). This was not a question of doubt but a question that expected an affirmative answer. The Lord God of Elijah opened the waters for Elisha, just as He had done for Elijah.

This is still a question after 3000 years and is one that needs to be demonstrated in your life and mine. Too many people have a very small view of God. They think of Him as Someone to run to when they are in trouble, and they call on Him only when they feel they need Him. Some are irreverent and border on blasphemy when they think of our God, the Lord God of Elijah, as the "man upstairs."

These low views of God lead to doctrinal errors. This is one reason why many people look to some kind of experience rather than to God Himself. They want some gift of the Holy Spirit rather than the Holy Spirit Himself. And low views of God contribute to a failure to apply Christian principles to conduct. Thousands of problems arise when we hold such views. We lack perfect obedience. We lack conviction of the sinfulness of sin because we do not see the holiness of God. We view Him as we do ourselves rather than as the infinite God to be held in awe and respect.

How can we describe such a God when we ourselves are finite? I can tell you some things I have learned about Him or have experienced. Then, for some things in this closing section, I am indebted to the late A. W. Tozer, who had a way of stating truth that is hard to improve on. His book *The Knowledge of the Holy* has been very helpful to me.

Elijah's God is the incomprehensible God; He is beyond human ability to fully understand or grasp. This is what Zophar meant when he said to Job, "Canst thou by searching find out God?" (Job 11:7). Our Lord said that no one knows the Father, except the Son (see Matt. 11:27). The Father can be known only through Jesus Christ our Lord (see John 14:6). Furthermore, no one knows the things of God but the Spirit of God (see I Cor. 2:11). Indeed, He is the incomprehensible God — but He is our God.

He is also the self-existent One. In science every effect must have a cause. There can be no result unless something produces that result. Some scientists honor God in their work, but others want nothing to do with Him. They try to eliminate God from His universe because they cannot account for Him or explain Him.

Nevertheless, every person receives life from God. It is a gift from God. Man is dependent on Him. God is self-existent, but we must depend on Him for every breath we take.

In his book Mr. Tozer illustrated this truth by reminding us of a sunbeam. When it is cut off from the sun, it simply perishes. So a person apart from God would perish if cut off from the benefits he receives from God. Elijah's God is the self-existent One, and He is my God.

Elijah's God is the self-sufficient One. I can give nothing to Him that He has not first given to me. Nothing is above Him or beyond Him. He cannot be promoted, neither can He be degraded. Dr. Tozer wrote: "Were all human beings suddenly to become blind, still the sun would shine by day and the stars by night, for these owe nothing to the millions who benefit from their light. So, were every man on earth to become atheist, it could not affect God in any way. He is what He is in Himself without regard to any other. To believe in Him adds nothing to His perfections; to doubt Him takes nothing away."* He is the self-sufficient and self-existent God, and He is our God.

God is not frustrated. He is never in need of our help and needs no defenders. He needs no one; yet when faith is present in a human heart, He will work through that person. Philippians 2:13 says, "For it is God which worketh in you both to will and to do of his good pleasure." But all our works, even those done in faith, can add nothing to God's self-sufficiency.

The God of Elijah is an eternal God. He dwells in all eternity. He has always existed. We are creatures of time and were created for eternity so that we could live with Him, but we had a beginning. God had none. Learn to know the God of Elijah. He is our God. Can you say for yourself, "He is my God"?

The God of Elijah is infinite. We are poor creatures, constantly frustrated and hemmed in by all kinds of limitations from within and without. Is it not wonderful and satisfying to turn to God, who is limitless in His powers and expressions? All nature has limitations, but God has none. His gift of eternal life is in Christ, and it is limitless.

The believer has the life of God in him. This is the eternal life we receive through faith in Christ.

The mercy of God is infinite. His love is measureless and boundless. God, as to His nature, is love, and because He is infinite His love is infinite also. This is Elijah's God. This is our God.

Elijah's God is immutable, or unchangeable. He never differs from Himself. He never varies from what He is. He never changes. He can never be more holy, nor can He be less holy, for He is holiness itself. God has always been what He is and will always be what He has been. God does not change. He is the God of Abraham, and Abraham's unchanged God is my unchanged God.

Elijah's unchanged God is my unchanged God. There is wonderful comfort in knowing an unchanging God in a

---

* *The Knowledge of the Holy,* by A. W. Tozer, Harper & Row Publishers, Inc., 1961, pp. 39,40.

changing world. "I am the Lord, I change not" (Mal. 3:6). With all our scientific knowledge, we have not changed God. The sad fact is that our scientific knowledge has not brought us any closer to knowing God. Only through the Word can He be known, and He is unchanging.

Elijah's God is omniscient; that is, He is all-knowing. Psalm 139 is a classic portion of Scripture dealing with this subject. This psalm can frighten us if we are running from God, but it can comfort us if we are being tested and afflicted. God knows all about us. And His knowledge about us is perfect. His knowledge has never been less so that He had to learn more. He does not need to learn anything, and He has not learned anything, for His perfect knowledge cannot be added to. In Isaiah 40:13,14 is this statement: "Who hath directed the Spirit of the Lord, or being his counsellor hath taught him? With whom took he counsel, and who instructed him, and taught him in the path of judgment, and taught him knowledge, and shewed to him the way of understanding?"

God knows all things. If knowledge could be added to Him, He would be imperfect and therefore could not be God. God never discovers anything, for He knows all things. He is never surprised or amazed, for nothing ever catches Him unaware. He knows us thoroughly. He is all-wise. In fact, the Bible says that Christ has been made unto us wisdom (see I Cor. 1:30). Elijah's wise God is our God.

Elijah's God is also the omnipotent God; that is, the Almighty One. He is all-powerful and sovereign. He has the right to do what He wants, and He has the power to do what He wants. In order to reign, God must have power. Because He is sovereign, He can do what He wants to do at any time, for He has the right to do so. But in order to do so, He must be the all-powerful God. This is Elijah's God, and my God. Do you recognize Him as your God?

While God has delegated a certain amount of power to His creatures, He has not lost any power in doing so. He is still the same God. Science discovers how God's power operates, but science does not add to God's power. We do not know what electricity is, but we are learning how to use it.

We do not know all that can be known about atomic power, but we are slowly learning how to put it to good use. These are powers in nature, and our God, the all-powerful One, is the God of nature.

Elijah's God is omnipresent. This simply means that God is present everywhere at the same time. He is close to everything and everyone. God is above and beneath and beside all things. He cannot be excluded from anything. But this does not mean that God and His universe are one and the same. He is separate from what He has created, and yet He is present with it at all times.

The climax of all of this is that Elijah's God is a faithful God. He cannot deny Himself. A failure to be faithful would mean imperfection. God is perfect; so unfaithfulness cannot occur in Him. We can count on Him to be faithful in everything He has promised to do for us. Since God is who He is, He cannot be different from what He is. He must remain faithful in all His words and acts.

But He is beyond all of this, for if we could describe God in human language, then God would be no greater than another human being. So He is all we have said and much more.

"O the depth of the riches both of the wisdom and knowledge of God! how unsearchable are his judgments, and his ways past finding out! For who hath known the mind of the Lord? or who hath been his counsellor? or who hath first given to him, and it shall be recompensed unto him again? For of him, and through him, and to him, are all things: to whom be glory for ever. Amen" (Rom. 11:33-36).

Elijah's God Still Lives

Elijah made a sacrifice
To offer to Jehovah;
It had been wet with water thrice,
Baal's sacrifice was over;
Elijah pray'd, the fire came down,
And lick'd the water all around,
And doubting ones believ'd and found
Elijah's God was living.

Elijah's God still lives today,
And answers still by fire;
My friend, just let Him have His way,
He'll grant your heart's desire,
Consume the sacrifice you make
And bid your slumb'ring soul awake,
And chains of inbred sin will break,
Elijah's God is living.

Elijah's God still lives today,
To take the guilt of sin away;
And when I pray my heart's desire,
Upon my soul He sends down fire.

—Rev. W. Grum

Scripture Index

15:17-18	102	18:18	57
17:45-47	68	18:19	9, 59
		18:20	62
		18:21	53, 62-64
2 Samuel		18:21-19:3	179
12:7	58	18:22-24	66
24:17	55	18:26-29	72
		18:36	79-80
		18:36-37	79, 178
1 Kings		18:37	81
17	8	18:38	81
17:1	12-13, 14, 15, 19	18:39	82, 98
17:1-4	22	18:41-42	87
17:2-7	176	18:42	89
17:3	45	18:43	89
17:6	25	18:44	93-94
17:8-9	30	18:44-45	89
17:8-16	176	18:46	96
17:9	31, 46	19:2	96, 99
17:10	31, 32	19:3	109
17:11-12	31	19:3-4	96
17:13	32	19:4	108, 109
17:14	32	19:5-7	115
17:15	34, 35	19:7	103
17:16	34, 35	19:8	117
17:17-18	41	19:9	121, 124
17:19	42	19:10	8, 109, 124
17:20-21	43	19:11-12	125
17:24	44	19:13	126
17:31-58	26	19:15	129, 130
18:1	46, 48	19:16	129
18:1-2	45	19:18	9, 134
18:3-6	49-50	19:19	136
18:4-13	9	19:20	137
18:5-6	54	21:20	140
18:7	52	21:21	143
18:9	52	21:23-24	143
18:10	48	21:25	146
18:12	52	21:27	143
18:12-13	52-53	21:29	143
18:17	57	22:34-35	143

Scripture Index

CPSIA information can be obtained at www.ICGtesting.com
Printed in the USA
BVOW05s1542180314

348029BV00004B/7/P